Thank You

Thank you to Ana (@earth222ana on TikTok) for sharing your story and vulnerability with your life experiences. Who would've known your TikTok on my FYP would've sparked this book idea.

Thank you to Michael Jaymes for being the fantastic editor that you are. I wouldn't have seen this all the way if not for you. Your suggestions helped me elevate the book beyond what I initially imagined.

Thank you to Simon Thompson for designing my book with my vision in mind and doing a great job at it.

Thank you to Casey Van Ommering for helping me structure the book.

Thank you to my parents for everything you've done for me. When I sit in that little corner, and you ask me what I'm doing, and I say nothing, this is what I was working on. I'm sorry I didn't tell you about the book until after I published it.

Thank you, Philemon, Mark, and Abdullah, for seeing the vision and making this happen. Only time will tell when you'll see your money back.

To the Webull gang who saw me work on this day in and day out, I appreciate and miss you all.

To Coach Ayosike, who inspires me and pushes me beyond my potential, thank you for all you've done for me.

To Tykwondoe, Dojo to the Moon 🚀 Your wisdom has helped me get where I am now.

I am forever grateful to Aba and Preach for the laughs, stories, and advice they gave me, which helped me find my purpose. AGAIN!

To ThinkTank Mafia, your guys' drive makes me want to be better than who I was yesterday.

Thank you Shimon Davis. Your videos have inspired a lot of what I wrote about.

Rokaya and Chimair, thanks for keeping my secret.

If I name one, I forget 10. There's no such thing as self-made. My friends. My family. Those who believed in me when I didn't believe in myself. I thank everyone who played a hand in getting me to this point—published author at 21. God is good.

Contents

CURE YOUR BRAIN ROT.

School Friendly

A GUIDE FOR MILLENNIALS, GEN Z, & GEN ALPHA TO FIND YOUR IDENTITY, PURPOSE, & "WHY"

PAPE K. DIOP

Cure Your Brain Rot: A Guide for Millennials, Gen Z, & Gen Alpha
to Find Your Identity, Purpose, & "Why"

Second Edition

©2025 by Pape K. Diop

ISBN: 979-8-9912977-2-1

Illustrations by Pape Diop and Simon Thompson

Designed by Simon Thompson

Introduction

Let's be real for a second. If you're reading this book, your attention span is probably cooked. The last time you read a book was for your English class, and even then, you SparkNotes'd it.

If it's not Instagram Reels, it's TikTok Lives. Twitter thinkpieces got you thinking the world is against you. Netflix docu-series captivate you to the point where one last episode becomes a seven-hour binge-session. Smoke sessions and Insomnia Cookie runs turn into solo sessions to take the edge off of life. And deep down, you know it's draining you. You're consuming instead of moving. You feel stuck, unable to focus, and like you're behind in life. That's what I call *brain rot*. The mental exhaustion you feel from living your life on autopilot, letting distractions control your life instead of living it with purpose.

You've probably tried to change, but it's hard. That 3 a.m. motivation can be so deceiving. One day, you're worried about where your life is headed. The next, you're up all night watching YouTube motivational videos, telling yourself you're going to make it. David Goggins makes you want to carry the boats. The Emma Chamberlain's of the world are inspiring your pretty girl vlog era. Kai Cenat subathons got you envisioning your own Twitch success, where every celebrity in the world wants to hop on your stream.

You're inspired. *No more TikTok for me. Never hopping on The Hub again. Quitting weed ain't nothing.*

Once you start attacking your goals, and that 3 a.m. motivation wears down, you're hit with the realization that the distractions are always there, the habits are tough to break, and before you know it, you're back to square one. The problem isn't just the habits themselves; it's that they've taken over how you think, how you live, and who you're becoming.

Taking control of your life begins with understanding and changing the habits that control you. It's so much more than reducing your TikTok scrolling, Instagram Reel binging, or your Hub addiction. It goes beyond. It's about creating a life you're proud of, living with the purpose that you've found for yourself. ▶

If you're reading this book, your attention span is probably cooked

I won't lie to you. 'Fanum tax' and 'sigmas' aside, curing your brain rot and creating a life you're proud of takes effort. In spite of this, you've taken the first step in the right direction. Every suggestion, every exercise, and every method provided is designed to be digestible and straightforward so you can apply it to your life and stay on the fast track to curing your brain rot.

I understand how addictive our devices and habits can be because I've been there. I know what it's like to be addicted to your phone, to distractions—to anything that pulls you away from where you're supposed to be.

It started with my phone. It was the first thing I saw when I woke up and the last thing I put down before I went to sleep. I didn't think much of it in middle school when the apps I used then were just as addicting as the ones now. Today, it's TikTok, but back then it was 'Do it for the Vine.' Roblox has a chokehold on the youth today, but my Roblox was Club Penguin and Poptropica. Nowadays, it's Wizz and Monkey, but back then, it was late-night chats on Kik and OOVOO that kept me going. My friend and I saw things in on those apps that no kid should. And yet, I look back at those times with a heart filled with nostalgia.

However, when I take off the rose-tinted glasses, all I see is regret. I'm faced with all the time I lost to my phone as it grew beyond an innocent pastime and a way to connect with my friends. It became pervasive. Conversations with friends and nights out were not enough to escape the reality of life getting harder as I grew up. My 'for you' page became my daily source of relief, adding a bit of humor to my day but taking away the possibility of a better future.

College was my breaking point. It's a place where you're supposed to find where you belong in the world, but I felt just as lost as when I came in. I dealt with the weight of social pressure—feeling like I had to be perfect, like I had to have everything figured out, even though I was barely holding it together. I've experienced the stress of trying to figure out my life after college, hiding my imposter syndrome, and losing myself to expectations that weren't even mine.

I wasn't living; I was consuming. I was living through my phone, watching life happen instead of creating my own path.

I remember one moment that really hit me—it was during my first year of college. I hit my first freshmen year slump. A mix of seasonal depression and uncertainty about the future: though those feelings weren't new to me, the intensity sure was. I couldn't get out of bed for a week straight. My roommate would check on me to no avail.

Eventually, amid my rotting away on TikTok, there was an itch in the back of my mind. *If you don't get up, you'll fail, which'll be more embarrassing than whatever you're going through. While my* fear of failure got me out of bed, I never addressed the root of the problem.

But when the freshmen slump turned into sophomore sorrows and junior year blues, the same issues kept presenting themselves, worse each time. Junior year was definitely the worst of them all—when the people around me were getting their lives together with internships while the one I had wouldn't give me a callback. When friends were hitting the gym and balancing school while I hadn't seen a weight in six months time. When my peers were achieving academic success while my grades looked like a relic of my past glory. Life knocked me down and made sure I stayed there. Fear was no longer a motivator; it was a sidekick to depression. I used social media as an escape for hours on end, to where my brain felt fogged and rotted every time I was done.

When I caught up with my best friend that summer, he told me, "You don't look like yourself. There's a certain sadness about you."

My brain couldn't even think of saying anything back. It was tired. The endless days of incessant scrolling cooked my attention span so badly that conversations with the people I cared about were exhausting. Twitch streams and doom-scrolling messed up my mind.

But that moment stuck with me. I realized that the brain rot I had been brushing off as normal was actually taking over my life.

Simple, everyday things, like catching up with a friend, had become mentally exhausting. I kept looking at life as a series of losses instead of celebrating the small wins.

"This can't be my life," I told myself. I wanted to be the uncle at the barbecue who always had a story to tell. I wanted to be the old man at the bus stop where every wrinkle around his eyes was an experience to share. I want my personality to have depth and my life to have purpose. ▶

It was the depression of my past and the fear of repeating it that fueled my studies, even in the midst of my own brain rot. After falling into the same cycles over and over, I started researching how technology affects our brains and how to break free from its grip. I took classes at my university that focused on the processes in our brains that drive our habits. I surveyed the people around me to understand how far the brain rot has spread. Through this research, I discovered that our phones are only one of many distractions our generation deals with. Other vices—whether it's weed, porn, or binge-watching—are just as destructive, even if we remain unaware of their impact.

The culmination of life experience and research has led to this: a personal guide on how to cure brain rot, taken from voices like you and me who want a life they're proud of and don't know where to begin. It's grounded in my personal experiences where anxiety, depression, and frustrations seemed to dominate, but on the other side came a stronger sense of purpose and identity.

The methods, exercises, and advice are created with you in mind. I'm not some outsider trying to empathize—I've lived it. I've watched as distractions and addictions consumed my life and pulled me further away from the person I wanted to be.

This is your chance to take back control. I'm not here just to help you quit scrolling TikTok or Instagram, entertain you with brain-rot references like "skibidi toilet" or "Fanum tax," or stop you from using other vices like weed or porn. My hope is to help you transform your life by finding your purpose and aligning your actions with that purpose. Curing your brain rot isn't about quick fixes—it's about lasting change.

If you're ready to stop living on autopilot and take back control, this is your moment. You will be challenged. You will be pushed. You will be frustrated, but if you stick with it, you'll see the results. This is your chance to beat the distractions, cure your brain rot, and build a life you're proud of.

A Word of Encouragement

I don't know how far gone you think you are or how mentally exhausted you've become. **If you're feeling like this is your last resort to change your life for the better, let this be the beginning of your change.** To be your catalyst. To free yourself from the chains of what controls you and finally take control of the wheel.

Life begins when you choose to live it, to take the reins and determine your direction. Hurt happens in every phase of life, leaving permanent scars once the damage has left its mark. However, that pain is also an opportunity to see the roots of trauma beneath, a chance to heal the damage with proper care and attention. Know that those scars will never go away. They'll act as a reminder, a caution sign to not let the same mistakes happen again.

If you want to break the cycle of poor choices, bad habits, or negative thought processes that limit your true potential, this is your first step. You will learn not only why your brain is rotting but how to get out of it. To find triumph through tribulations.

I believe in you.

What is Brain Rot?

When I say "brain rot," I'm referring to the gradual decline in attention span, critical thinking, and meaningful communication caused by excessive exposure to social media and digital trends.

When people talk about brain rot, they refer to the impact social media has on their day-to-day lives. For instance, your younger sibling randomly and unironically says "Fanum tax" or "I just rizzed a level ten gyatt," in a conversation. How every time you trip on something in front of the "bad jawns," you think about the "aura" you lost. How your girlfriend says "period," "big back," and "baddie baddie shot a clock," every other sentence. Seeing someone fall off and calling it a "generational crash out." Instead of giving a beautiful woman a normal compliment, you instead say she's "2016 Lebron James," or "3 a.m. water." (If these terms look like gibberish to you, don't worry; that's a good thing.)

At the moment, it's funny and seems harmless. But if you really think about it, it's fascinating how quickly social media can cause us to adopt new words, ultimately changing our brains. The word *mysterious* is now "aura farming." *Congratulations* is now "W's in the chat." It's not called taking care of your face and body anymore; it's now "mewwing" and "looksmaxing." Bodegas in New York had to suffer through tourists and locals asking for a bacon, egg, and cheese the "ocky" way. And please. Please. Do not get me started on the word "gyatt." It's alarming how it can become our personality so quickly.

But this is just the tip of the iceberg. Brain rot refers to more than just social media; its impact is more serious and severe in nature.

To put it simply, brain rot is when your mind affects your physical state, making it harder to do everyday tasks and responsibilities.

I was a person who used to light up a room, but over time, I tried to exit conversations quickly—it just took too much of my mental energy. My friends say they used to feel mentally sharp before they started smoking weed. Now their brain just runs off Red Bull and vibes. Maybe you relate to experiencing a lot more of those moments of "Damn, I should've known that!" It's as if your critical thinking is fading. ▶

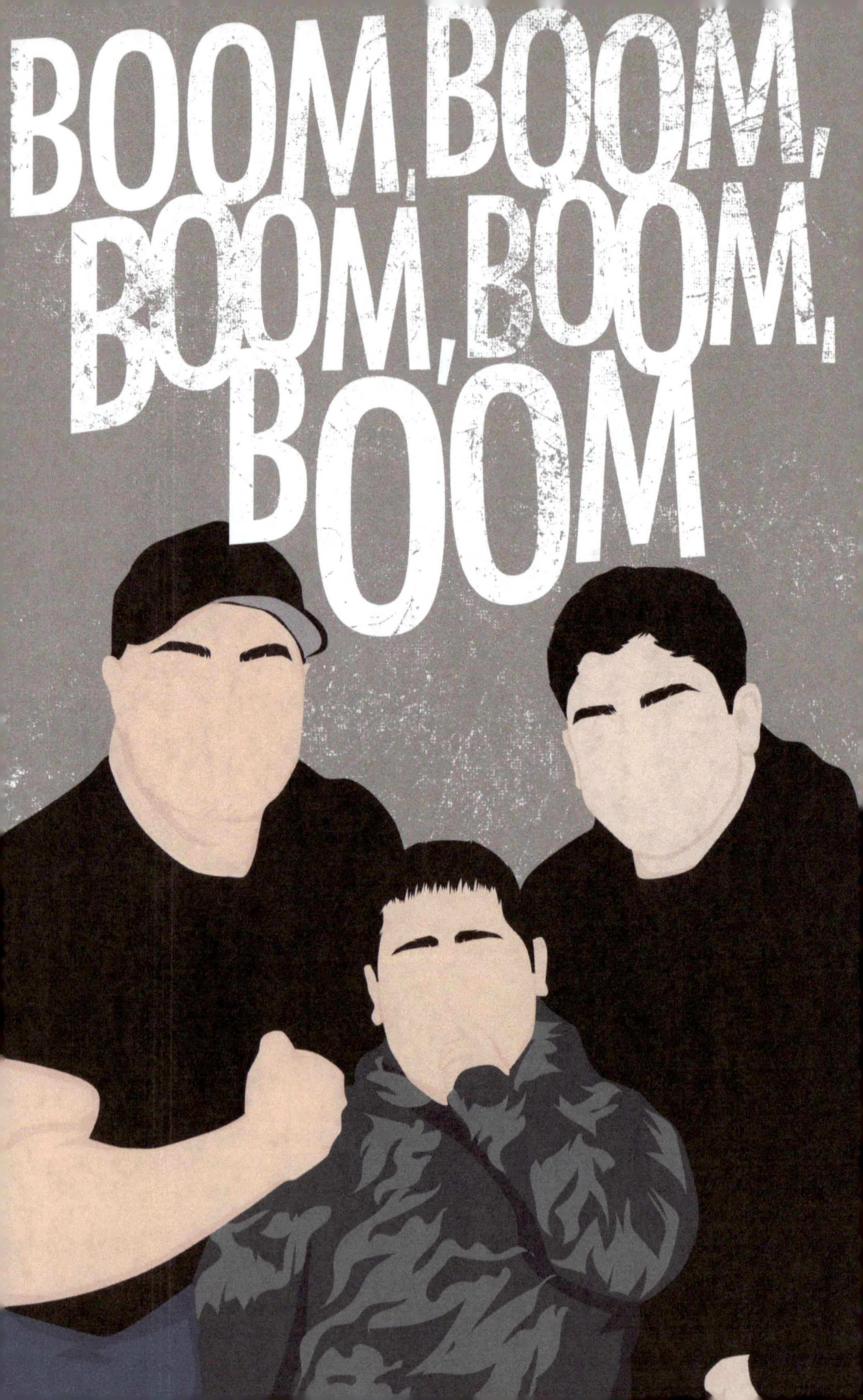
BOOM, BOOM,
BOOM, BOOM,
BOOM

Brain rot is that slow-growing moss creeping over a forgotten garden statue. It's barely noticeable at first, but slowly, it transforms your once vibrant mind into a relic of its former self. People experiencing brain rot often find themselves with terrible memory problems, mental exhaustion, and engaging in fruitless conversations.

This is the real brain rot I'm talking about. As in, your brain feels like it's legitimately rotting. I'm sure you've noticed how it affects your day-to-day life. You likely have goals, ambitions, and dreams but don't have the blueprint to achieve them. Ever wonder why? Brain rot is a result of the issues holding you back. Cycles of bad habits stop us from progressing, taking ownership of our lives, and becoming the people we want to be. It's not as easy as saying "no" to your vices once. It requires a lifestyle change, a mental shift from negative trains of thought. Otherwise, the all-too-familiar cycle persists.

We've all been victims of it. I remember when I first realized the cycle. I kept asking myself questions like: Why is it so hard to break away? Why do I keep falling back into old habits? Why do others seem to have an easier time sticking to their tasks without distractions? ▶

FEELING SAD ABOUT WHERE YOUR LIFE IS AT WANTING TO
CHANGE IT

FALL BACK INTO DESTRUCTIVE HABITS (WEED, SOCIAL MEDIA, CONTENT)

TAKING ACTION TO **FIX** YOUR LIFE

FEELING LIKE THE EFFORT IS TOO
MENTALLY DRAINIING

It largely has to do with how your brain is developing. The patterns we fall into, especially between the ages of twelve and twenty-five, can have a lasting impact on our ability to focus, resist temptations, and maintain mental clarity.[2]

Neuroplasticity

Your brain is highly neuroplastic during this time, meaning it's incredibly sensitive to change and adaptable to your surroundings and experiences. Neuroplasticity is the brain's ability to reorganize itself, forming new neural connections throughout a person's life.[3] This adaptability allows you to learn new skills, adapt to changes, and recover from injuries more efficiently, though the opposite is also true. This means that negative habits and environments can easily be ingrained into you.

When we see someone do something stupid, we joke and say, "Their prefrontal cortex didn't develop all the way." There is truth to this joke. Your brain is hypersensitive to the information it's receiving and the actions you take. If you're always smoking, scrolling, or gooning, you're slowing down this developmental process and taking away from your future.

Does this sound familiar?

Let's take a closer look at some effects brain rot can have. Take note of how many relate to you.

• Your Brain Feels Fried: Like a Literal Fog:
Your thoughts feel thicker than the fog in Los Angeles skies. It's almost like a white noise in your brain, distracting you from thinking. There's a TV static feel to it, representing your blank state of confusion.

• No Motivation
Your goals remain wishful thoughts instead of manifesting into reality. The fog turned to quicksand, stopping you from moving in the right direction. There's this perpetual feeling of exhaustion that comes with brain rot that makes you feel like you're too tired to do anything.

• Lacking in Conversation
You don't have anything interesting to say. You follow conversations without taking the lead. Other people have vibrant conversations, while you wish your brain could just come up with something instead of short-circuiting. Weird and awkward pauses are becoming more commonplace in your convos than in any real dialogue.

• Nothing Comes to Mind Anymore

Once a beautiful canvas of thought, your mind is now a cesspool of nothingness. It feels as though your brain is turned off, and you're moving through life on autopilot. Moments where you blank—whether it be in person, watching a show, or during a class—become more common.

• Loss of Critical Thinking

When you constantly scroll and consume—not reflecting on each article, video, picture, or piece of information you come across—you find yourself adopting other people's opinions instead of creating your own. Your critical thinking is limited to simple reactions like "damn, that's crazy" or "No way" without delving deeper into your thoughts. Developing a point of view is difficult for you to formulate. It's not your choice to be indifferent; rather, your brain struggles to engage with others' opinions with strong reasoning behind your thought process.

• Loss of Identity

Not only do you feel yourself morphing, but you're actually losing who you were. You're adopting thoughts that are not your own without even thinking about them or considering the consequences of those thoughts. You don't even recognize yourself when talking to other people as if you're somebody else. You feel like you've lost any interesting, redeeming qualities about yourself.

• Low Energy/Exhaustion

Mentally exhausted from the brain fog, your body doesn't want to cooperate. Outside of getting out of bed, going to school or work, and eating, you can't muster the energy to do much else. Your bed turns into your sanctuary, and more often than not, you feel like you're betraying your future by wasting valuable time. ▶

Low Energy/Exhaustion

Your Brain Feels Fried, Like a Literal Fog

Loss of Identity

Opting for the Easy Way Out

Addicted to Your Phone

NOTHING COMES TO MIND ANYMORE

Lacking in Conversation

No Motivation

Loss of Critical Thinking

Opting for the Easy Way Out

• Addicted to Your Phone

The only thing better than that 3 a.m. water is that dopamine boost you get every time you check your phone. You must have it on you at all times. You spend hours and hours doom-scrolling, watching videos so that you'll forget about what's on your agenda.

• Opting for the Easy Way Out

Valuable things require too much effort. Your brain tends to prefer the path of least resistance. Rather than hitting the gym, you opt for Ben & Jerry's. Instead of an early bedtime, you scroll all the way till the ass-crack of dawn. This tendency worsens as your mind becomes more clouded, leading to a loss of control over the habit.

If you answered yes to any or even all of the above, you're not alone. A 2022 survey of about 1400 teens in the US reveals that 97% of them use the internet every day, up from 92% in 2014-15. The Pew Research Center found that 46% say they use the internet "almost constantly."[4] It's all too common; the allure of immediate gratification is overpowering. Acknowledging that you have this tendency in the first place is step number one toward overcoming it. Our brains are lazy by nature, and every day, we must fight against our very instincts, our distractions, and the temptation to take the easy way out.

If any of those descriptions gave you a visceral reaction, whether anxiety, nervousness, shock, sadness, etc., know that's a good thing. That means your brain is doing what it's supposed to be doing—working. You are tangibly aware of how brain rot is affecting your day-to-day.

You may still be blaming yourself for the brain rot you're experiencing. You might wonder: Is it my fault that my brain feels like L.A smog? Am I just being lazy? Lacking motivation? Wanting nothing out of life? The truth is, it's not as simple as laying all the blame on yourself or external forces. Yes, social media and other addictive technologies are designed to pull you in, often without you realizing it, but at the same time, you're the one holding the reins. Whether you want to blame yourself for getting sucked in or point fingers at those TikTok interns keeping you tapped in through the algorithm is beside the point. ▶

Looksmaxxing

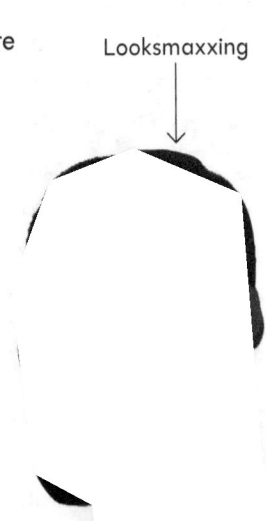

The responsibility to take back control of your life rests with you. Awareness is the stepping stone of change.

It's your responsibility to understand what controls you and what holds you back. These problems stem from deep-rooted issues. Any root issue you have can typically be grouped into three categories. What are they? **Trauma, escapism, and self-sabotage.**

Those words are deep. They make you stop and think for a minute. Or two. Or ten. Let's break them down for a bit now and explore them more in-depth later.

Escapism

is when you seek distractions or run from difficult realities and emotions by immersing yourself in something else. You don't want to think about how your future is coming at you fast, so you'd rather lose yourself in your "for you" page or roll a joint to escape that thought. It's about running from what's uncomfortable.

Trauma

is one reason people tend to escape their realities. It involves unresolved emotional wounds from the past, which can leave you coping unhealthily with what traumatized you.

Self-Sabotage

happens when you get in your own way—whether it's through procrastination, fear of failure, or making choices that you know will harm your progress. These mechanisms sometimes work hand in hand and reinforce one another, creating a cycle that's hard to break.

While these roots often explain why someone can't break free from an addiction or destructive habit, it's important to recognize that not all addictions begin here. Your childhood & teenage years, for example, are a time of exploration and acting on impulse. We fall victim to curiosity, peer influence, or the desire for a good time. The beginnings are the most innocent of times. We saw smoke sessions as a way to socialize and used the munchies as an excuse to crush entire boxes of Dominoes by ourselves. Social media was a place where we posted and laughed at memes and videos that are now considered Facebook mom humor. You probably weren't searching for the Hub when you found it. A friend told you about it, and you let curiosity get the best of you.

That curiosity grows into a habit and blossoms into a negative feedback loop where the innocence of what was disappears while the harsh realities of why you indulge in your vices set in. Smoking stops becoming social and starts becoming an escape. Social media scrolling becomes clockwork for you, while the minutes turn to hours, and the day ends with nothing to show for it.

Whether you suffer from one, both, or all three, you won't find a solution or inner peace unless you strengthen the three pillars of yourself: **your identity, your purpose, and your "why."**

Briefly, your IDENTITY is who you are and who you choose to be the moment you step outside of the house. Either your raw and unfiltered self or a persona you've created. Do you choose your true interests, desires, and upbringing or the ones that are imposed on you by others? Your identity has to be in alignment with your purpose. ▶

We fall victim to curiosity, peer influence, or the desire for a good time

With each wave, you will learn to navigate the tides of your inner world, taking back the parts of yourself that have been lost at sea

Your Purpose is what you were born to do, your intrinsic motivation to make a difference to the people around you, and what you want to gain more in this life than anything else. What skills you were born with, and how do they help others.

Your "why" is simple. Why you do what you do, and who do you do it for? Why do you care so much about being the next influencer? Your "why" is the true motivation behind your goals and not the reasons a society told you to have.

These three pillars of yourself are chained together, with your identity serving as the most integral chain. Before you know what you are meant to do and why you do it, you must first know yourself. If the identity link is broken, your purpose and your "why" falls with it. If you develop your purpose and your "why" before your identity, the identity link becomes too weak to hold the weight of the others, bringing everything crashing down.

Unraveling the layers of our behaviors isn't just about taking a break from Instagram or taking that T-Break. It's about truly getting to know yourself. The use of weed and social media, to cope with life's difficulties aren't just passing habits formed in a void. They're artifacts of our youth, reflecting what has remained unsolved and unmet. They are the echoes of our adolescence that we've neglected. The source of your inaction more than likely is due to unresolved trauma or negative learned behaviors from your past that have prevented you from exploring who you are.

After uncovering these roots for possibly the first time, you will feel uncomfortable. You will feel overwhelmed. You will feel emotional. You will ask questions. You might not get the answers you're looking for. It will be awkward. It will hurt. You will experience these emotions in waves, and just like the ocean, you will flow through these feelings, sometimes drowning in their depths, other times finding yourself washed ashore, exhausted but still breathing. Yet, with each wave, you will learn to navigate the tides of your inner world, taking back the parts of yourself that have been lost at sea. Facing these memories, thoughts, and emotions is a step toward permanent change. Intimidate your fears with confidence, and they will retreat in the face of your dreams.

Identity

Mel Robbins once said, "How you see yourself is how you see the world." It's a statement as true as time, and yet, is a truth that remains undiscovered by most. One of the most cliché but underrated drivers of action is purpose. Notice how I didn't say motivation. Motivation is fleeting and temporary, but purpose is grounding.

Success deals with more than just a decision to stick with a goal. It has to do with your purpose and your identity. It deals with who you are, what you believe about yourself, and why you stand for these beliefs. Success follows those who believe in their potential, those who don't see doubt as a reflection of their potential but rather as a form of motivation, pushing them toward the confidence they've always had within. If you truly believe in your success, you pave the way to achieve it. You are the product of your beliefs, and your life becomes a reflection of the stories you tell yourself. Those who see themselves as capable and worthy will always prove it to themselves.

Failure follows those who believe it about themselves; success follows those who dare to believe in it.

If you tell yourself every day that you're going to succeed, you've already succeeded. You've encouraged yourself instead of giving in to your limiting beliefs. Believing you are successful not only changes how you see yourself, but motivates you to take the steps to reach your dreams. You must act based on who you can be rather than the misconceptions of who you think you are. What you need is identity. And purpose. And use your "why" to keep you going. That internal motivation to act must come from within, and that belief must be fueled by you and you alone.

Purpose

Though purpose alone won't drive your action, it's important to understand that without it, you fall into this cycle of brain rot. And it's not that you are without purpose. It's that you haven't taken the time to flesh it out and really set in stone what it is that you want to do.

Your purpose is not in the dropshipping course you impulsively bought to make money. Your purpose is not what your parents want for you. Your purpose belongs to you. And though you may have a similar purpose to somebody else, no two canvases are painted the same. You have your own way of contributing to the world that no one else can because you are one of one. You are 100% unique in comparison to anyone you know.

Yes, we have goals. Yes, we have ambitions. But what is it rooted in? What drives them? Is it a destiny we want or a destiny imposed?

Those are some soul-searching questions. I'll ask you this, though: What is your "why?" Why do you wake up every day? Why do your dreams captivate your heart and mind so deeply? Why? Uncover this truth or risk a life unfulfilled.

Why

Once you determine your identity and purpose, your "why" and success will naturally follow, only if you're honest about what truly drives you. It won't appear all at once, but as you grow in both areas, you'll find that you own your motivation instead of it being outsourced to you. Your "why" becomes yours and yours alone.

Who were you as a child? Who were you until you learned the dos and don'ts of your personalities? Until you molded them to the expectations around us? Were you the class clown always sent to the principal? The adventurous kid always exploring the woods and alleyways like a stooge? An expressive kid who shared stories on Wattpad? We often look back at who we used to be and cringe. This is a good thing. But think about what part of yourself you had to suppress to get here. Go back to when you were a kid and try to think of all the character traits you had. Your true desires and passions. That's where you can return to find yourself and then work back to where you are now.

Your "why" fuels your purpose, and your purpose pours out from your identity. When any of these are weak, you become vulnerable to your vices. A fragile identity often signals low self-esteem, a lack of confidence, and a diminished sense of self-worth. It means you haven't fully grasped who you are or what you're truly capable of. If your "why" is weak, it means you don't deeply understand what truly drives you. And a weak purpose is the result of a weak "why." Strengthen your "why" to solidify your purpose and in turn, fortify your identity—because when these are strong, you are unstoppable.

Putting the Pillars Together

You need purpose and identity to overcome the cycle of brain rot. Solidify your "why," and you can see your vision through the obstacles and the roadblocks. This process takes time. Purpose and identity come from a deep understanding of who we are and exposing uncomfortable parts of yourself that you've probably kept hidden all these years. However, you can't jump straight into asking yourself why without uncovering the symptoms that guide your bad behaviors. What are these symptoms? Your insecurities, your fears, your doubts, your hurts, your anxiety, and the trauma that seems to always win hide-and-seek. Exploring these through inner work helps to paint a picture of who you are, which fortifies your "why." Once you know yourself, you'll start to see why you fall into destructive patterns and make the conscious decision to change them.

Knowing yourself and being in tune with your identity is not limited to the benefits you see internally. The confidence you gain from knowing yourself can be felt by those around you. As smooth and confident as we think we appear, our words, body language, gestures, and physical disposition allow others to spot our confidence or insecurities from a mile away, obvious to everyone but ourselves. How you walk into a room, how tall you stand, how much eye contact you make, the tone of your voice, and what you choose to say are all direct reflections of how you see yourself. Your presence speaks volumes before you even utter a word. People can sense the authenticity in your demeanor, and this either draws them in or pushes them away. ▶

Some attributes transcend beyond attitudes and behaviors. They are personified.

Confidence and trust go hand in hand. To be confident about an outcome means you trust yourself to get there. To be confident about a relationship means you trust yourself to give your all, regardless of the outcome. The same goes for identity. Understand that people will trust you only if you trust yourself. There is a protective aura that surrounds people who trust in themselves. People will naturally follow you into paths unknown because they believe in you and what you stand for. They can see that you possess the courage to lead with conviction and the wisdom to inspire them through the darkness of their own problems. You have the potential to possess power that influences people solely through the belief you have in yourself. Your confidence is their comfort. Your self-security is their sanctuary.

People around you are always watching how you act, react, present yourself, and engage with the world. Your past behavior will give them an impression of what you are going to do. If you were known as the person who half-assed assignments, barely got by in school, and put in little effort, their expectations will align with these qualities. The good news is that you can change. Over time, people will see the change in you and naturally be drawn to the person you're becoming.

To do this, you need to know your identity, know your purpose, and know your "why." If you can lead yourself with conviction and confidence, people will follow you regardless of your past or regardless of any mistakes you've made. Start asking the hard questions about yourself. Start looking at why you do the things you do. Seek feedback from others. Grow as a person. To get rid of the brain rot, you must change yourself first. Only then can you change your habits.

This change won't come easy. It's easier to wake up and ignore the fact that your identity is not yours. It's even harder to spend every day committing yourself to finding it. Think about the alternative, though. A life where you doom scroll for hours on end, smoke until the grabba is dust, and use content to escape reality. A life where you don't trust that you can build a better reality for yourself. A life where the idea of success and the fear of failure is more terrifying than the sanctuary of complacency you've built around you. A life where you tell yourself if you never try, you'll never fail.

Craft My Motto

Write a sentence, phrase, or quote that you'll live by that feels true to you. Don't force it. You can create one or find one. Let it find you...

My Motto

I'm just a man of the people, not above but equal. And for the greater good I walk amongst the evil
– J. Cole

Your Motto

....

....

....

....

Identity Tree

- On the roots, write what values ground you and give you strength.
- On the trunk, core aspects of your identity that shape your life.
- On the branches, what are the dreams and goals that extend from your identity.

Dopamine

The Elephant in the Room

Thank you Dr Anna Lembke and Ali Abdaal for providing the framework for this chapter.

Let's begin with a widely misunderstood part of our lives. Dopamine. A widely misunderstood neurotransmitter in the brain. The internet has coined this term "dopamine detox," as a way to reset your brain from the damage it received from all the distractions in your life.

Let's get one thing straight. Dopamine Detox is not a thing. Detox is a bad way to describe resetting your dopamine levels. A detox is a noun and a verb meaning the following:

Detox (noun)

A process or period of time in which one abstains from or rids the body of toxic or unhealthy substances; detoxification.

Detox (verb)

Abstain from or rid the body of toxic or unhealthy substances.

You cannot detox from dopamine. If your body detoxed from dopamine, you'd be dead. Your body requires dopamine to remind you to do the things you need to function. Eat, drink, sleep, etc. It plays a key part in rewards and motivation. Here's the process of how dopamine works in your brain.

1 Dopamine operates in two primary ways in the brain: tonic transmission and phasic transmission.

Tonic

Random release of small amounts of dopamine. This is your baseline. Think about this as the white noise you put on when you go to sleep or the sounds of the river when you're by a lake.

Phasic

2 Represents a surge of dopamine in response to specific cues or rewards, signaling an event above the baseline level. Think of this like seeing a person you missed that you weren't expecting to see.

3 **Scenario: College Admissions**
Imagine you are a high school senior who has applied to several colleges. Your baseline dopamine levels are stable due to the regular, continuous effort you put into maintaining your grades, extracurricular activities, and college applications (tonic transmission). ▶

Tonic

You receive an email notification from one of your top-choice colleges regarding your admission status. This notification acts as a cue, triggering a phasic release of dopamine because you anticipate a potential reward in the form of an acceptance letter. From here, there are 3 outcomes:

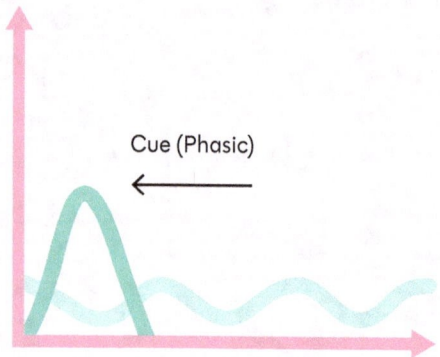

Cue (Phasic)

4 Acceptance from Top-Choice College (More Than Expected)

Scenario:

You applied to several prestigious colleges and expected to get into a good but not your top-choice school. Instead, you receive an acceptance letter from your absolute top-choice college.

Dopamine Response:

This unexpected acceptance causes a significant surge in dopamine levels (phasic transmission), leading to feelings of excitement, accomplishment, and relief.

See how the reward is so much higher than the cue?

Cue

Reward (Phasic)

5 Acceptance from Expected College (Exactly as Expected)

Scenario:

You applied to several colleges and expected to get into one of your top three choices. You receive an acceptance letter from a college that was within your expected range.

Dopamine Response:

The acceptance matches your expectation, so there is no additional dopamine release beyond the initial cue from receiving the email notification. Your dopamine levels remain stable.

Dopamine is not released because your expectations were met

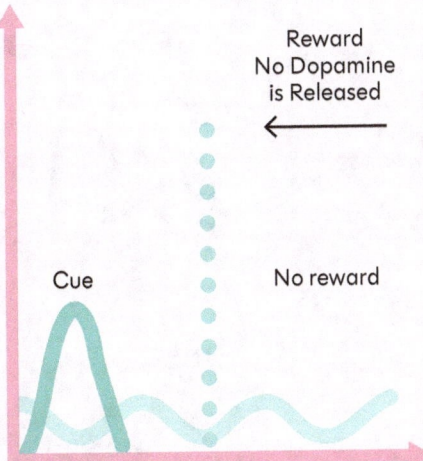

Reward
No Dopamine
is Released

Cue   No reward

6 Rejection from Top-Choice College (Less Than Expected)

Scenario:

You expected to get into one of your top-choice colleges but received a rejection letter instead.

Dopamine Response:

The rejection is less positive than expected, resulting in a decrease in dopamine levels. The reward prediction error (getting rejected instead of accepted) leads to a drop in dopamine. ▶

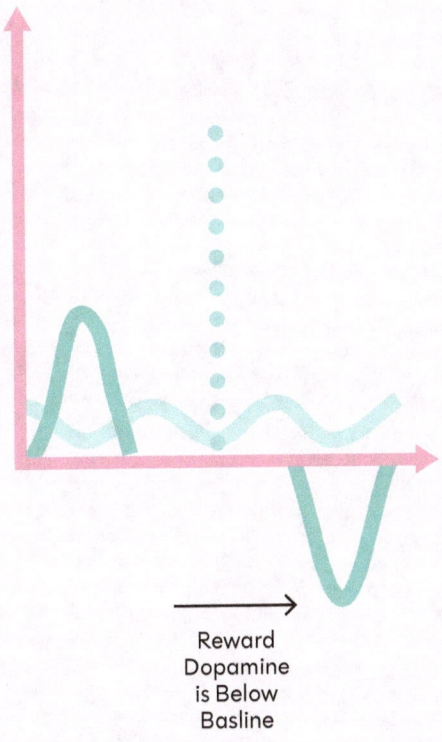

Reward
Dopamine
is Below
Basline

7 So What is your Problem?

Your problem is you're messing up your baseline dopamine levels.

Tonic

This is your baseline.

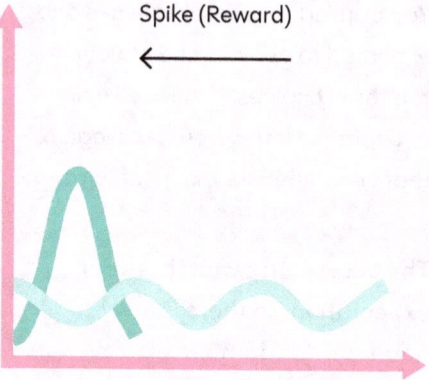

Before you're addicted, the spikes of dopamine (phasic) is above the baseline, making you feel good.

Spike (Reward)

But, the more you abuse the things you're addicted to, you increase your baseline level of dopamine (Tonic).

Baseline Before

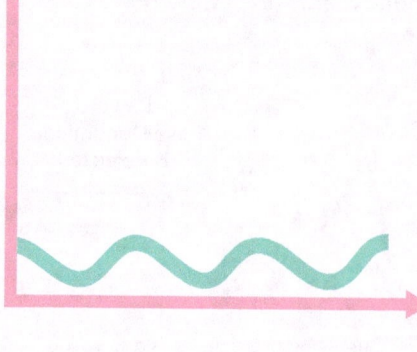

Baseline Now

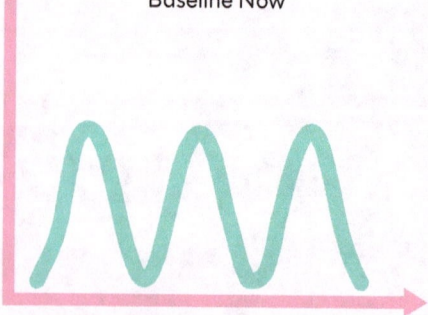

This means 30 Minutes on 2K isn't enough to make you feel good anymore. You need 2 hours. That TikTok binge goes from 2–3 hours to 5. One pint of Ben and Jerry's salted caramel core isn't enough to satisfy the cravings. You need "The Tonight Dough" flavor to go with it too.

Formally speaking, you need more to feel what you once felt because you increased your baseline, therefore increasing your tolerance.

8 This is called a Dopamine Defecit State.

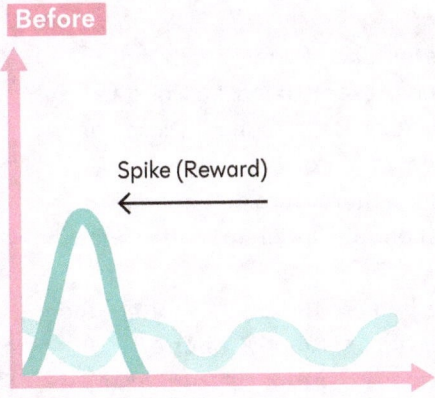

Before

Spike (Reward)
←

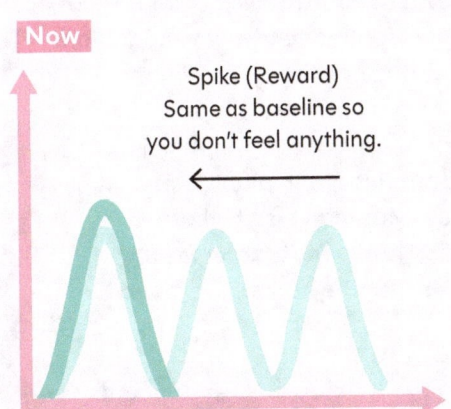

Now

Spike (Reward)
Same as baseline so you don't feel anything.
←

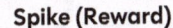

Spike (Reward)
You have to now push yourself here to feel anything pleasurable or rewarding

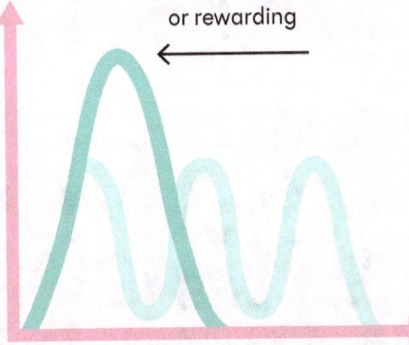
←

This state makes low-dopamine activities (e.g., reading, walking) less enjoyable and contributes to feelings of anxiety and depression. That's why when you watch that movie, you gotta check your phone. When you go to McDonalds, you engage in big back activities and order well above what you know you should eat.

According to Dr. Abdaal, in order to reset your phasic and tonic levels, you have to detox NOT from dopamine, but high and addictive dopamine inducing activities. For a minimum of 30 days.

Now that the elephant has been addressed, let's get into how it plays into your vices.

Causes of Brain Rot

Brain rot has multiple causes. I'll be covering the three main causes in our generation.

Marijuana

DISCLAIMER

You might argue that vaping is the bigger epidemic of our generation. Chances are, you know someone who can't go without their mango-flavored vape pen as they cough up whatever's left of their lungs. Back when I was growing up, it was all about Juul Pods. Today, it's Zyn, Blu, and Vuse. I completely share your concerns about the damage vaping has caused and how deeply it's rooted in youth culture.

The reason marijuana is the focus instead of vaping is that the stigma around vapes has always been present, at least as long as I can remember. We used to call them "nic sticks," "cancer sticks," or even "raspberry death." Depending on your crowd, lighting one up often came with a look of sha§me. Sure, there were defenders, but they were few and far between. Most people understood they were inhaling something harmful.

Marijuana, on the other hand, has been so thoroughly normalized that raising an eyebrow about it feels almost taboo. Criticize it, and you've got about ten seconds to leave before you're put on a T-shirt. Let me be clear: I fully acknowledge the medicinal benefits of marijuana and support its use when prescribed to alleviate conditions like chronic pain, anxiety, or other health challenges. But what I've observed in its recreational use is far from harmless. It's damn near destructive. The unbridled defense of its casual consumption is fueling a wave of misinformation about this green plant.

It's crucial that we strike a balance. Marijuana isn't inherently evil, but it's not without its risks either. That's why it deserves to stand alone in this conversation—because the narrative around it needs to evolve.

Yup. You guessed it. Mary Jane. Pot. Zaza Pachulia. Ganja. Doña Juanita. Reefa. The devil's lettuce. Joint. Spliff. Chronic. Doobie Doobie Doo. There are many names for the world's favorite leaf.

Third to caffeine and alcohol, there isn't a drug more socially accepted than marijuana. Casual marijuana consumption even surpassed casual alcohol consumption in 2024![5] Not only is it accepted, but excessive use is incredibly normalized. Cyphs and hotboxing are a regular occurrence. My friends always kept a plastic bag handy, ready to cover a smoke detector when the time came.

Marijuana gets a lot of positive publicity because people don't often associate marijuana with brain rot. It's harmless, right? Though a lot of people see a problem with the recreational use of weed, the grabba defenders are at large and ready to smack the fire out of you if you say anything about their precious green plant.

If you want a laugh, tell your stoner friend that weed isn't good for them and watch them talk like they got a PhD in plants. "It's just a plant." "It's natural, it can't hurt you." "It comes from the ground!" Yea, so do cocaine and heroin.

Casual use of marijuana does not receive the pushback that it probably should within our generation.

Imagine you put a dollar in a piggy bank every time someone in the world claimed they weren't addicted to weed. Consider the number of people who claim their use of marijuana is not a problem—whether to their parents, their friends, or concerned individuals. Think about the feens in your friend group and how they behave without their daily eighth. How much do you think you would make?

By the end of the month, you'll probably have vacation homes in every country. It's condos in Colombia instead of combos at Wendy's.

I had an "I can quit when I want to" friend who smoked every day. He would've put the fear of god into Snoop Dogg if they ever crossed paths. If he's the NBA, Wiz Khalifa is junior varsity. I always told him I dreaded the day he went without his green nug. One day, I saw him looking a bit irritated. His eyes were bloodshot with grocery bags under them, so I asked him what's up. He told me the plug was out of weed and that he couldn't try his mango backwoods wraps. It was enough to bring his mood down the whole day. Hilarious but tragic.

It's more than just THC in, Problems Out. Marijuana affects your brain in ways you likely don't even realize. From memory issues to feeling slow, detrimental effects occur in both short-term and chronic use of weed.

How Weed Causes Brain Rot

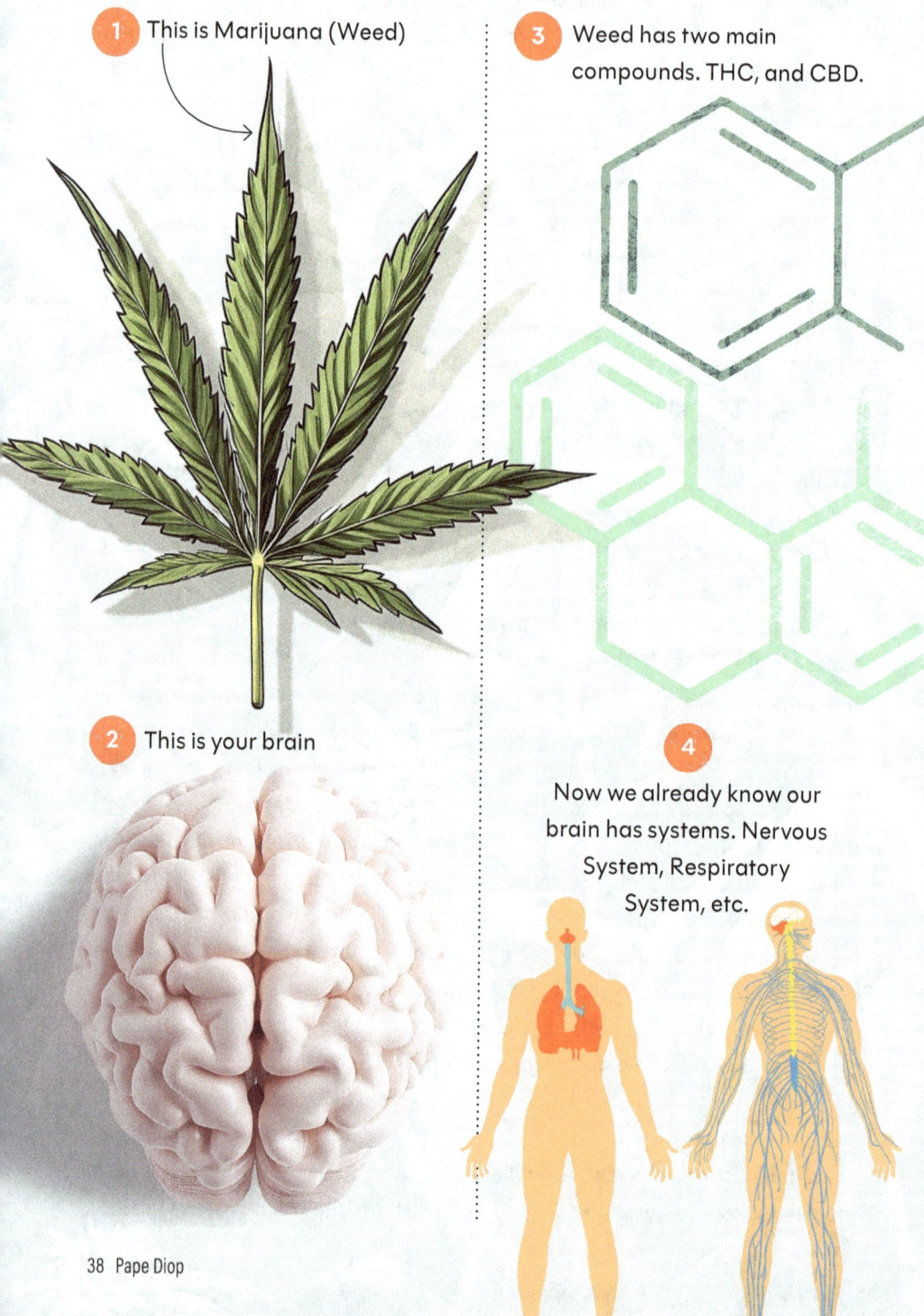

1 This is Marijuana (Weed)

3 Weed has two main compounds. THC, and CBD.

2 This is your brain

4 Now we already know our brain has systems. Nervous System, Respiratory System, etc.

5

However, you've probably never heard of the Endocannaboid System.

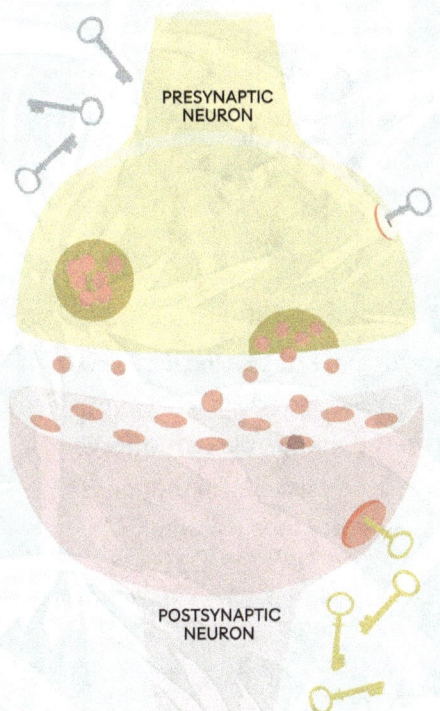

PRESYNAPTIC
NEURON

POSTSYNAPTIC
NEURON

6

The endocannabinoid system is a network in your body that helps regulate processes such as mood, memory, pain sensation, and appetite.

7

Your brain has endocannabinoids. These endocannabinoids are tiny molecules that bind to receptors in your brain, which helps to regulate yourself.

8

Think about it like connecting two puzzle pieces, one piece being the endocannabinoid and the other piece being the receptor, but everytime the two pieces connect, something different is affected, like your mood, appetitie, etc. ▶

9 Everytime you smoke or ingest weed, THC is carried from your blood into the brain.

10 Think of THC like an endocannabinoid. In your brain, it binds to receptors. Like the puzzle above. Once that THC is binded to the receptor, you release dopamine.

11 A lot more dopamine than usual is released which makes you feel euphoria, relaxed, and even accomplished. This happens every time you smoke.

12

However, over time, as you keep smoking, your brain starts to produce less of its own endocannabinoids. Which means when you are sober, less dopamine is being produced. The high dopamine in your brain when you smoke becomes the new normal. Which means when your brain releases normal amounts of dopamine, it doesn't feel like it's enough. You start to crave weed more to get those dopamine levels back up so you can feel happy and euphoric again. So when you take a break from weed after smoking it so much and you fall into a depressive rut, this is why. But it's not only responsible for dopamine. THC also affects parts of the brain responsible for memory, which is why you've noticed over the months and years of you smoking, you're starting to have the memory of a goldfish.

Basically, a consistent use of weed makes you dependent on it to achieve a higher level of dopamine. Consequently, if you smoke a lot and then take an extended break, it will likely cause you to fall into a depressive rut. Your brain won't have the ability to produce the natural dopamine levels it once produced immediately. It will take time to recover and start to restore a healthy baseline of dopamine again.

Weed is not only responsible for dopamine imbalances; the THC in weed also affects areas of the brain responsible for memory, particularly the *hippocampus*. You may have noticed by now that your memory is cooked, resulting from months or years of smoking.[6] You'll be two or three TikToks in, forgetting the one you just watched. Marijuana may be socially accepted, but don't be deceived—its impact on your brain and life can be significant, especially if it's become more than just an occasional habit.

Why should this matter to you? If you find yourself a *wake-n-baker, a backwoods bandit, or a grabba gremlin*, you're only slowing yourself down from accomplishing any goals you have in life. If you are dependent on weed for your day-to-day function, you will not progress or succeed at a notable level. That blunt is the devil on your shoulder telling you everything is going to be okay. Stressed about your future? *Smoke me. I can show you a better one.* Now, all that time you could've spent working on your goals is spent working on those pre-rolls. Can't sleep? *I can show you a type of peace you've never felt.* Over time, weed dreams turn to insomnia, and now you can't sleep without melatonin pills. It doesn't end here. Imagine one day you meet someone who can change your life and put you in a position you've always dreamed of, but your brain is so fried you can't bring up one interesting thought. You're there physically, but mentally, you're a thousand miles away. The opportunities you lose because you're chasing a high? You'll never get them back. Each hit may feel like a moment of relief, but in reality, it's stealing your potential.

You'll never know the opportunities that'll slip you by because you decided to chase a high or the people who will cut you off because of how its taken over your life. A perpetual high isn't a life you're truly experiencing; it's a life where your feelings are dictated by the next hit, where weed takes the lead while you follow. Every hit takes away from who you could be. A creative. The fun auntie that lights up the function instead of the one that's cranky without her blunt. ▶

A philanthropist that's a legend in your local community. Think back to a time before you smoked, and look at yourself now. It's worth considering if you are really living or if you're just getting by in a fog of smoke.

I had a good friend growing up named Sebastian. He was a legend, but only the way an elementary kid could be. During lunchtime recess, he could bend a soccer ball like Beckham, run laps around us like Bolt, and make it back in time to piss off our History teacher. If he wasn't in parent-teacher conferences, he was napping at In-School-Suspension, driving the principal insane.

His lash-outs were hilarious to us. Every class was a Netflix comedy special. We never stopped to ask what fueled them. We didn't know about the nights he spent staring at the ceiling, trying not to cry. About the hole his father left when he passed away when he was six. That kind of loss shapes you, even when you don't know how to put it into words. His mother, who abruptly became a single parent, lashed out at her children because of the stress. School was his only outlet to express himself, and soccer became his peace. That expression was a way to hide his pain behind a smile.

In middle school, he found another way to cope. This time, it was with a friend. Her name was Mary Jane. She was green, wrapped in a brown dress, ready to relieve any problems in his life. Every lunch break, every after-school hangout, Mary Jane was there. He smoked every day, to the point where a teacher caught him hotboxing in the bathroom and enrolled him into a drug rehabilitation program. That didn't matter because he brought Mary with him everywhere he went. She helped him forget about the pain from his father's absence and the sting of his mother's words.

High school was nothing more than a two-year stint for him. He dropped out, and with that, he dropped off my radar. News about him came in bits and pieces from mutual friends. His mom had kicked him out, they said. He was working odd jobs to scrape by, couch hopping at friend's homes and college dorms. I'd search for him online every now and then, but his social media was silent.

Around my sophomore year of college, my phone buzzed. It was a Snapchat notification—a friend request from Sebastian. I was surprised to see it, given that I'd been trying to reach out for years. We talked for a bit, and he told me how he was starting to get his life together. He applied for his real estate license and was getting back into soccer, training with his cousin, who was a coach for the local teams. He said he found a religion that aligned with him, strengthening his relationship with God, and found his way to the mosque every Friday. Hearing him talk like that made me proud. It felt like he'd finally outrun the ghosts that had chased him all his life. We didn't talk often after that, but I checked in now and then. I wanted to see him win. Until one day, I sent him a message. It sat on "delivered" for weeks, then months. I figured he was taking a break from social media focusing on himself.

I ran into a friend in passing, and I asked how he was doing. His whole mood changed. "Oh, Sebastian. He passed away. It was a fentanyl overdose."

I was floored. I couldn't believe it at first. I saw fentanyl overdoses on the news all the time, but it was the first time it hit this close to home.

He wasn't that much older than me. Only twenty years old. He wanted to put his family in a better position like me. He wanted to know what a college experience was like. Life had other plans, though. It put my mortality into perspective. Here is a man who had a lifetime of family troubles, started to turn his life around, and passed away because Mary Jane introduced him to Snow White.

I spent days replaying it in my mind. ▶

He had so much potential. A potential he committed his life to finding. He tried to change the cards he was dealt but was robbed of the chance to change his life. Sebastian had spent his short life trying to outrun his demons. For a while, it looked like he might win, like the times he won against us in recess. Even though we could never catch up to him back in those days, life eventually did. All I'm left with now is the memory of a friend whose story ended before it ever had the chance to begin.

Weed is not just a plant. All it takes is one bad hit, one bad trip to the plug, or one laced bag, and your life ends before it even begins. Even with the 'cleanest' strands, you pay for it in plenty of other ways. I've seen the most creative people, individuals who could even rival the late Virgil Abloh, turn into a blank canvas. Friends who haven't had a sober day in years, numbing their pain with weed.

You have the power to put down the blunt and pick up where your life left off. To grow into the person you're destined to be without the influence of Mary Jane's whispers. Take the driver's seat back and learn how to phase this vice out of your life.

What do you smoke?

Joint   Blunt   Spliff

Track Your Triggers
For the next 7 times you smoke, log how you felt before you smoke and how you felt after.

1 Before?..
   After?..
2 Before?..
   After?..
3 Before?..
   After?..
4 Before?..
   After?..
5 Before?..
   After?..
6 Before?..
   After?..
7 Before?..
   After?..

Social Media

If you've scrolled on TikTok until that very sweet woman pops up on the screen, saying, "Found yourself scrolling again?" your brain is probably cooked. And no, don't worry, you're not the only one. We are a generation affected by the good, the bad, and the ugly of the all-consuming world of social media.

The first time I downloaded Instagram was in 2012. I was a nine-year-old kid with an iPod Touch and unrestricted internet access. Great combination. My first Instagram post was a picture of me with a Capri Sun in my mouth, holding up a peace sign, and I captioned it "just chillin." My mom used to shave me bald, so the comments called me a milk dud, but I found it more funny than anything else. Back then, people posted anything they wanted, and I wasn't an exception. They had to know my Flappy Bird high scores. Everyone had to know I was watching *Everybody Hates Chris* while eating Cocoa Puffs on a random Wednesday in 2013. If I got new Jordans, Insta would know before my parents, and they were the ones that bought 'em.

When Vine was the new craze, forget about it. Everybody wanted to be King Bach, DeStorm, and Drew Gooden. Vine references became ingrained in our personalities. Were you really living if you didn't practice your whip and nae-nae in the mirror? Did you really throw something if you didn't say "Yeet?" You couldn't bring bad shoes to class unless you wanted someone to record them and say, "What are thoseeeeee!" Everytime I saw a "Road Work Ahead" sign, I thought, "I sure hope it does." If you had a hat on when Bobby Shmurda came on back in 2013, it was law that you launched it to the sky and hit the Shmoney Dance, screaming, "about a week ago." You knew that hat was never coming back, and you had to be okay with it because the moment was bigger than you. I used to hide my iPod under my pillow and watch those Vines until the asscrack of dawn, pretending I was sleeping when I heard footsteps outside my room. ▶

Found yourself scrolling again?

2.5M

67.9k

173.8k

@takeadeepbreath

Scrolling like you're unemployed again?
You've been on here for 10 hours. Take a
deep breath with me and go get a job.

At this point in my life, my attention span wasn't completely cooked, but it was cooking. Those six-second videos started to do irreversible damage to my ability to pay attention, but I'd be lying to you if I said those Vines weren't worth the consequences.

Nowadays, that initial excitement is gone. Social media has evolved. Instagram stopped becoming a place to capture a moment in time, but rather planned moments where every detail has to be perfect. On my feed, birthday pictures are no longer innocent family photos of your mom smashing your face into a Baskin Robbins cake. It's a photoshoot behind a white studio backdrop with a photographer charging $650 an hour. Twitter stopped being a place where you see the funniest jokes known to man. It's filled with blue-check rage baiters spewing the most racist rhetoric alive for a monthly check.

These social media platforms that formed our identities and brought us so much joy became a cesspool of ads, attention farming, and manipulative practices aimed to make you never look away at your phone. We're old enough to have seen social media be the hero and lived long enough to see it become a villain. A villain with no face but endless reach. What made social media so nostalgic and pure has vanished in the pursuit of perfection.

Despite the initial excitement of socializing across the world, we now know social media is more than just a virtual space to be social. It's a place to learn and engage, but also a platform to spread disinformation, hate, bully, and, perhaps most pervasively, create a realm of constant comparison. A once-innocent idea has been commercialized to the highest bidder. Marketing companies spend millions of dollars every year creating content for social media users like you and me to keep us hooked. The prized and coveted social media algorithms have people by the leash, having them see exactly what they care about the most. The concept of social media addiction is relatively new to the medical and behavioral health world, and researchers are still assessing it for conclusive evidence. It's like we're the guinea pigs of this long and destructive experiment. Despite the lack of definitive research, we don't need to look at the results any further than our phones. When was the last time you grabbed it? The last time you thought about it? How much screen time do you put in each day? Did you check your post over and over to see how many likes you got? How many Tiktok beefs are you caught up on? What did your ex repost about you this time? No matter where we go, it *has* to be on us. ▶

We can find any justification to check it. You feel a buzz. You hear that ringtone. You finally got a text back after you sent that long paragraph to your ex, only to read, "Yea, I'm not reading all that. I'm happy for you, though. Or sorry that happened." You can read this, along with all the studies in the world about the detrimental effects of social media, understand exactly what it does to your brain, and still go back to it.

Your mom was right. It is that damn phone.

But why? Why is it so addicting? I gotta see what was posted on TheShadeRoom. Why is Miranda Cosgrove on Kai Cenat's stream? David Dobrik made a coming back to YouTube video? Why isn't Duke Dennis nerfed yet? I can't miss out. I want texts. I want calls. She's gonna text me back, you'll see. Why is it so hard to get rid of?

I'll tell you why...It's addictive by design. Social media companies have made a fortune training their algorithms to hijack your attention span. They've dialed in *exactly* the content you want to see based on your search history, what you show interest in, how long you spend looking at a post, and who knows what else.

I got younger siblings glued to the screen on Roblox with one computer while swiping on their iPads at the same time. I've seen moms at movie theaters give their kids an iPad with headphones because they can't pay attention to what they came to see. I've seen kids at Korean BBQs celebrating their birthdays with their families while watching a Mukbang on their mom's phone. Glad we don't have it that bad, right?

I beg to differ! If anyone is to be pitied for wasting precious time, it's us. The youth. The younger generation. We are *consumed* with it. *Driven* by it. *Motivated* by it. The iPad kids of our time sit in the back of the class and shop on Aritzia or Porsche.com, customizing cars not to purchase but purely for the love of the game.

Social media seemed to start with more noble intentions, appearing as a harmless tool and a means of communication. At first, it was advertised as a way to connect with friends and family, to bridge worlds from people across the globe. Suddenly, you could update others about your exciting life and engage online to make plans or catch up.

Long gone are the days when social media was a harmless tool. It's been developed and monetized against us. Virtual hugs and validation have replaced genuine connection. Something once so simple has morphed into the very brain rot that you've tried to overcome.

Ways Social Media Affects You

Doom Scrolling

We've all done it. We've all been persuaded by the phone's gravitational pull. Just one app. Just two. Just five minutes...ten...an hour...two. Who's counting? Maybe you opened up TikTok around 9 p.m. and soon became consumed with the endless stream of content. Next time you glance at the clock, it's 3 a.m. You're shocked by how much time has passed. Then you're startled by the gentle chime of an advertisement with a soothing voice asking, "Found yourself scrolling again?" The reality sinks in—six hours have slipped away unnoticed, lost in the entertainment abyss of social media. This phenomenon we call doom scrolling is a testament to the addictive nature of apps and digital platforms. It's compulsive, the urge to keep scrolling, fueled by a mix of curiosity, FOMO (fear of missing out), and the relentless pursuit of that next dopamine hit.

The effects of doom scrolling aren't as apparent as first. Maybe a couple of laughs. Trying to find the TikTok that'll have the group chat dying. Stocking your saved posts with funny but relatable videos that you'll come back to later. But once the reality of lost time sets in, so does the realization that you're not where you want to be.

The consistent exposure to an overwhelming barrage of information, images, and opinions from your "For You" page can lead to sensory overload. Our brains struggle to process the sheer volume of Tiktoks and Reels that we watch in our 6-hour binge session. An average TikTok in 2023 was 39.5 seconds.[7] If your TikTok binge session was an hour, then you watched 91 TikToks on average (but we both know the number is probably more.) How about three hours on TikTok? That's 273 TikToks on average. That's 273 videos on 273 different topics that your brain is trying to make sense of. Because of the sheer volume of content you consume, your brain is left feeling like hazy fog. In a state of 'rot,' so to say.

The overwhelming BARRAGE of information, IMAGES, + opinions from your page can lead to sensory OVERLOAD

Addiction and Brain Rewiring

Social media can lead to psychological addiction as well as brain rewiring due to the elevated levels of dopamine associated with social media use. Studies show that 40% of internet users ages 18 to 22 feel like they're addicted to social media.[8] Even though this isn't substance-based addiction, brain scans show similarities in the brain regions associated with drug dependency.

Specifically, brain scans of people addicted to social media display degradation of white matter in areas responsible for emotional processing, attention, and decision-making.[9] **Simply put, think of white matter as a network of cables that helps your brain communicate. Less white matter means these connections are slowed down, affecting your memory, attention, and emotions.** Forgot your keys when you left the house? Is your bestie mad at you because you forgot her birthday? Do you blank when someone asks you what day it is? Your white matter is being chipped away at.

When I was in middle school, I had a terrible eye infection. I thought it would pass, but my mom insisted I go to the hospital. Man, was she right. My ophthalmologist, who I've been seeing for my whole life, took one look at my eyes and called in a specialist.

That specialist took one look at my eyes and called in another specialist. That specialist took one look at my eyes and called in the senior specialist. The senior specialist took one look at my eyes and said, "Mother of god."

I had a hole in my retina. Had I come in a day or two later, my eyes would've been cooked! He told my mother, "Tomorrow is the weekend. I don't typically work, but it's very important that I come back and take a look at your son's eyes again. Take out a piece of paper, take down my number, and call me when you arrive. It's 678-999-8212."

Saturday morning, I'm back at the hospital. My eye's no better than the day before. My mom is at the receptionist's desk, telling her we have a special appointment.

"With who?" she asked.

My mom says, "Oh, I wrote it down. It's right here." She's fumbling with her purse, trying to find the note with the doctor's name and number, until a realization hits her. She left it in her other purse.

"Ma'am, unless you have a doctor's name or number to confirm, I can't help you."

I looked at the receptionist with my swollen shut and infected frog eyes and said, "678-999-8212."

My mom was looking at me with awe. "How did you remember that?" ▶

I honestly couldn't tell her because I didn't know. The receptionist confirmed the appointment, called the doctor in, and I was able to get some medication that saved my eyes.

All this to say, I'm ten years removed from that moment in time, and I look back at myself with envy at how easily I was able to remember things. Even the things I wasn't trying to remember. Sure, I was younger then, and memorization comes more easily at that age. But comparing it to now, when I can barely remember my class number halfway through the semester, I definitely miss that mental sharpness. All those years of doom-scrolling couldn't have made it better, either. I try my best to take care of my mind now, but that white matter degradation—the quiet cost of social media—has impacted me in ways I couldn't foresee.

Impaired Multitasking Abilities

Contrary to popular belief, heavy use of social media does not enhance multitasking abilities but rather impairs them. Research comparing heavy media users to others shows that those who frequently switch between tasks, such as toggling between work and social media, perform significantly worse in task-switching tests.[10] Think of your brain like a browser with a bunch of tabs open. You're on the tab with algebra open because you have an exam tomorrow. A distraction, a notification, or a TikTok is like popping open another tab. Instead of your brain using its power to get that degree and make your momma proud, it has to divide its power, make sense of the Kai Cenat clip you just watched, and keep all of those tabs open. And here's the kicker—unlike a computer, your brain doesn't have an instant "clear all tabs" button. So, every distraction lingers, making it harder to focus when you actually need to.

Dopamine

Every time we check our social media accounts and see something we like, we experience a temporary spike in dopamine, similar to how we feel when we eat or engage in other pleasurable activities. Just as with other sources of dopamine hits, our threshold for enjoyment increases the more we spend on these apps. That's why "just one more video" never really means just one more. This cycle of craving and temporary satisfaction can lead to a form of psychological addiction. Our brains become rewired to constantly seek out these dopamine boosts, similar to substance addictions.

Tell me if this sounds familiar. You're up. It's late. You're either on the game, or you're watching those "pop the balloon" videos with Arlette. You suddenly think "I need to lock in and do something with my life. It's time for me to finally change. It's time for me to get back to me."
You spontaneously hop onto YouTube, searching "How to get rich," "How to be motivated," or "How to change your life." You're all psyched and ready to go at 2 a.m. You decide; I'm going to get up earlier and work out! Maybe you take a cold shower before going back to bed, wake up at 5 a.m. to go on that run, or impulsively buy that gym membership.

What happens next? Your desires meet resistance. This is harder than I thought it would be! "I was ready to go last night, but now I'm tired." I don't feel like doing that today. Now what? You're back at square one, leading to negative thoughts about yourself and your efforts. You feel unworthy of success, as if it's just not meant for you.

You pick that phone back up. Abuse the dopamine levels in your brain as you doom scroll again. You wait for motivation to strike, but only after you exhaust yourself with social media's endless content. A vicious cycle.

In and of itself, social media is not a bad thing. It may look like the culprit to all your problems, but once you learn how to engage with it, you realize social media is not the end-all, be-all. You have to acknowledge that your inside life doesn't have to match people's outside lives, the one they portray to the public.

Caption Like It's 2016

Paste your own picture ot draw below

Insert your caption here

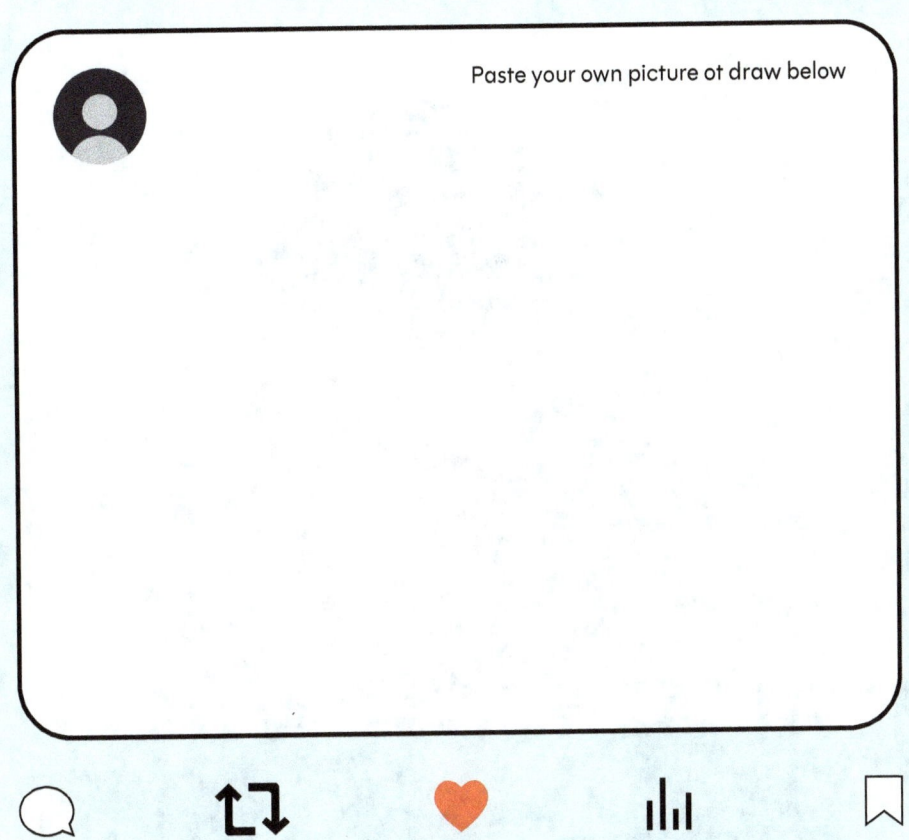

Paste your own picture ot draw below

Iconic Vines of Our Time

Everybody Say Sausage Keep it Going

Oh Don't Do it

Drop It Like
It's Hot

FRE SH A VOCA DO

Hurricane Tortilla

Look At
All Those
Chickens

If You Know,
You Know.

Ya Yeet

About a week ago

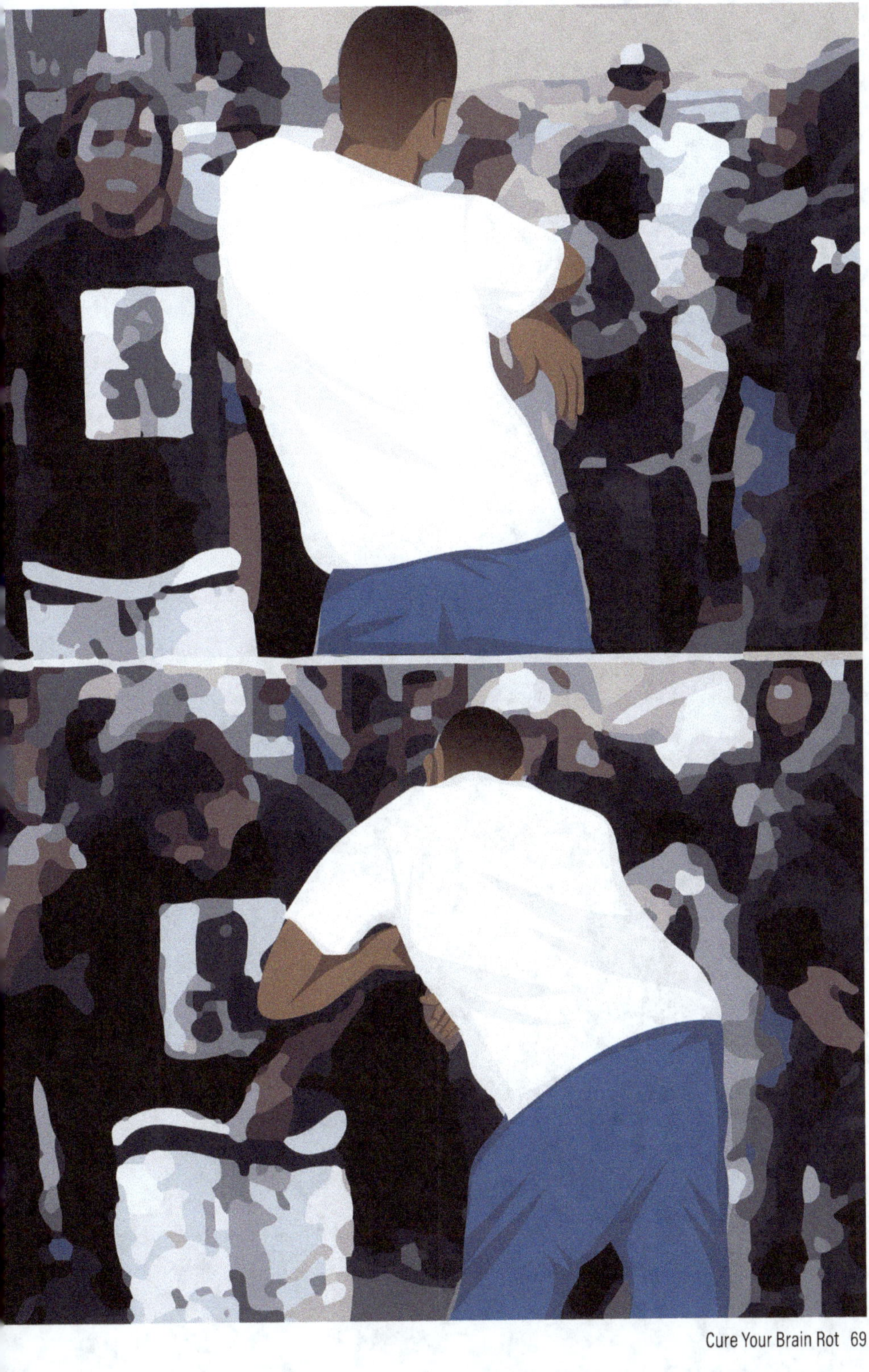

The Big Three

When I say the Big Three, I'm not talking about Drake, Cole, and Kendrick or Lebron taking his talents to South Beach with D. Wade and Chris Bosh. I'm speaking about the problems that are likely the cause of your brain rot: **escapism, trauma, and self-sabotage.**

You don't have to stay stuck in your brain rot. You don't have to smoke constantly, scroll endlessly, or entertain the Hub. You can break those addictions. There's a life so much greater than the highs and lows of rotting your brain.

So, why do we give in to our vices, and how can we turn that around?

Escapism

I remember the day I planned my escape. I just couldn't take it anymore. I was tired of constantly being blamed for things that weren't my fault. Why was it that every time the dishes weren't done, my mom blamed me instead of my sister? Why was I the one in time-out? Seven-year-old me was seething. So, I did what any rational child would do: I went upstairs, emptied my sister's Jonas Brothers backpack, packed my clothes, and decided to run away. By "run," I mean I walked two city blocks before the fear of being alone sent me back home. Escape failed. These days, escaping reality isn't as dramatic as packing a bookbag and storming away in child-like fashion. It's as simple as picking up my phone. If my mom irritates me now, I can just bury my face in social media and drown out the noise. If you think about the "destressors" in your life, they're often just coping mechanisms for the parts of your reality that feel negative—or that you perceive as negative. And these de-stressors act as an escape from this negativity. Boss burning you out? No problem. You have a friend named Mary Juana waiting for you after your shift, always reliable. Girlfriend getting on your nerves? The Hub is there to help you "take the edge off," and she will never argue with you. These substances and media forms let you escape the bad parts of your reality without ever addressing them. Even the word "escape" implies that what you're running from feels like a prison. For some of us, that prison is our daily routine, built from mundane tasks that drain us of energy. For others, it's a lack of motivation and discipline that traps us from developing a routine we're proud of. These escapes offer a temporary sanctuary but ultimately take away from our long-term potential. Whatever the reason may be, what you're running from is fueling the behavior that's causing your brain rot. Your brain will always choose the path of least resistance and the path of most relief. *Why do I want to escape? Why do I feel like I have to give in to my vice?*

Running from what needs to be done

Let's consider a common scenario. You've got a Biology presentation due two weeks from now at 11:59 p.m. Two weeks in school terms feels like two years, so you don't give it any mind, but it still lingers. In the midst of your TikTok scrolling and YouTube video essay binges lies a whisper in your mind, reminding you that this project is no small feat. As two weeks turn to one, and one turns to five days left, the reality of the situation sets in. You become committed to finishing this task and tell yourself you're going to cut off distractions and focus solely on the project. You start off well and feel good about yourself for starting a bit early. "The mitochondria is the powerhouse of the cell." "White blood cells destroy viruses." You're on a roll.

Slowly but surely, the work started to feel a little boring. It's not stimulat-ing enough. The mitochondria aren't giving you the energy you're looking for. Your brain is itching for something more, so you pick up your phone and indulge in some TikTok brain rot to satisfy that itch. At that moment, you hear a voice in your head telling you to lock back in. You proceed to get back to the job, but then you get that notification from your three-person group chat (the one with a crazy name). You click on it, then you blink, and two hours have passed. You have nothing to show, but you tell yourself, "Hey, I got this. I started early enough, so I'll still finish on time."

A day goes by. Day two flies by, then day five. There it is. The deadline. You've got three hours. The adrenaline starts to kick in after you realize how much time has passed and you have nothing to show for it. You decide to buckle up, put your phone on DND, and get to work. You're hypnotized by the sound of the repetitive keys. You finish and turn in your project, only to see that you half-assed it. In one paragraph, you even wrote, "Waste is removed by our bodies from our three kidneys." But hey, at least you finished! You're mentally exhausted by all the effort you had to put in at the last minute to turn in an "okay" project. What do you do next after all that work? You go back to your only source of solace—your phone.

There it is again. Your phone in hand. You wasted all that time on it just to turn in a mediocre project. There's a lesson somewhere in all of this, but it's buried under the relief of hitting submit. The stress of the last-minute scramble disappears as quickly as it arrives. You probably didn't even stick around long enough to see the Canvas confetti celebrate your work. This cycle repeats itself. The stress of the task fades the moment you complete your work, and the next deadline feels too distant to worry about now.

What I described is a classic case of procrastination. Everybody likes to joke that they are master procrastinators, but what is really the root cause of delaying tasks? Dr. Itmar Shatz, creator of the successful blog *Solving Procrastination*, describes it as a stress response to either your environment or your future responsibilities.[14] Most people assume procrastination comes from laziness when it's really an avoidance of stress. It's not the thought of the task itself that brings you anxiety. It's the feelings *associated with* the task—feelings such as fear of failure, self-doubt, and a sense of being overwhelmed—that trigger the stress response. This is what triggers your avoidance behaviors and the cycle of procrastination that you can't seem to crack. At the same time, procrastination and stress can be a self-reinforcing cycle. For some people, procrastination can cause stress but isn't triggered by it, while for others, stress itself can lead to procrastination, which only makes their anxiety worse. This cycle can continue indefinitely, with each instance feeding into each other until something breaks the loop—like a project deadline, for instance, forcing you to act in spite of your feelings.[14]

These emotions create a mental barrier, making a task seem more difficult than it really is. This is coupled with the fact that it's in our nature to choose the path of least resistance. Evolution shows that our ancestors, faced with survival, needed to conserve energy whenever they could. Those who spent less energy on unnecessary tasks were more likely to survive and pass on their genes. Today, it seems as though that innate wiring is still prevalent. We're predisposed to choose the path of least resistance, even if it's not the best course of action.[15] Procrastination and choosing the easy road temporarily provides some relief, but this short-term escape results in long-term consequences. You start perpetuating a vicious cycle that's hard to break.

There are several processes that occur in your brain when you feel the need to run away from responsibilities. The main one most people fall victim to is Temporal Discounting.

Temporal Discounting

Temporal discounting is the cognitive bias that causes us to prioritize immediate rewards over future benefits. We convince ourselves that how uncomfortable we feel or the effort of finishing a task is worse than the long-term benefits we'll gain from completing it. This bias makes procrastination an appealing option; it allows us to avoid our immediate negative feelings.

When given a plate of food, it's common to eat the veggies first before moving on to the main dish. Why? The rest of the meal tastes so much better once the pesky vegetables are out of the way. This type of delayed gratification is a micro example of temporal weighing, where you prioritize long-term pleasure over the immediate benefit of the main dish. Or, to put it simply, finishing the asparagus before you dive into the steak. On a small scale, it shows how finishing what is less desirable first is more rewarding than choosing immediate comfort that will ultimately come back to bite you.

Every day, you're faced with a choice—prioritize future success or immediate comfort. If you choose temporary relief, it will stop you in your tracks every time. No motion. No progress. You may be excited by the thought of success, but there is a disconnect between what you want and what you're willing to do to achieve it. The thought of all the work it will take to get there makes you stressed, and uncomfortable with being uncomfortable.

You want that six-pack or that "snatched bod," but the thought of 6 a.m. wakeups and Chloe Ting workouts just wasn't doing it for you. Instead, you'll go to Wingstop and get yourself a ten-piece with cajun corn, binging *Grey's Anatomy* and *Power Book II* in your H&M flannel pajamas, going from a waist size 28 to a 32.

You may have dreamed of a mountain of cash, erasing you and your family's financial burdens for good. The thought of putting away 35% of each paycheck, however, just hurts your soul. What do you do instead? You took yourself to TikTok Shop and got a fake Essentials Hoodie with some Denim Tears jeans, walking around the mall shooting 0/10 from the field. Then you sparked in the parking lot in your Honda (that smells like backwood guts), talking to your friend about how "I gotta make it" and how "my life just ain't it."

Every time you engage in this type of behavior, you're wasting time rather than developing your potential success. If you continue this temporal discounting, what will you have left? Regret. Disappointment. Wasted years. The remnants of a life that never truly began.

Masking your reality

This type of escapism stems from dissatisfaction, but it manifests in two distinct ways. On one hand, we use our vices to escape a reality that we perceive as negative. This can be a bad job, bad grades, credit card debt, or anything in your life that brings you stress and anxiety. On the other hand, we escape to avoid facing what's missing from our lives. Be it the dream house, the dream car, or true financial freedom.

While these ideas overlap, they can lead to different behaviors. Escaping a bad job or stressful situation by lighting up that joint is an immediate response to discomfort. A temporary mental reset to recover from a stressful day. Escaping the lack of companionship or meaningful relationships by using The Hub, for instance, is a deeper reaction to long-term dissatisfaction. Both forms of escapism may offer relief at the moment, but they can prevent us from addressing the underlying issues.

Escaping to mask what's missing from our lives

"When you invite envy into your life and into the lives of others, you'll pay for it in ways you can't control." – Aba Atlas

This quote resonates deeply with the modern struggles we face in a social media-saturated world filled with constant comparisons. If you spend hours consuming the snapshots of other people's lives, the trap of envy is all too easy to fall into. You see others living out the dreams you have for yourself, enjoying the attention and recognition from success that seems to evade you. It becomes harder to appreciate what you have when you're always moving the goalposts, focusing on what you lack instead of valuing what's already in front of you. Your self-worth is affected, making you feel inadequate and fueling a cycle of feeling that you're not enough.

The price of inviting envy in your heart is steep. It distorts your perception of reality. *Everyone else has it better than me!* You might turn to smoking to numb the feelings of inadequacy. You might dive into Instagram to avoid your own life's challenges. Actions driven by envy provide only temporary relief when they really only exacerbate the underlying issues. The more you envy others, the more compelled you feel to seek out peace in harmful habits. You become entrenched in a cycle of despair and avoidance. Envy not only steals your joy, it causes you to vicariously live out other people's dreams. ▶

Dreams that you believe are out of reach for you.

Harmful habits and unlived dreams go deeper than envy. These are centered around your belief about your reality. Your belief about yourself. Your identity. Your perspective on life profoundly shapes your experiences and emotions. If you believe your life is lacking or that you're somehow less than others, you are actually inviting feelings of inadequacy, sadness, and frustration. These negative feelings drive you to seek out other ways to escape or numb the pain.

Years ago, when I was on the road to finding myself, I was faced with the reality that I wasn't where I wanted to be in life. It led me into a spiral where I didn't celebrate the small wins and started viewing life as an accumulation of losses. These losses were a combination of efforts and attempts I made to better my life that ended up failing in vain. In the lowest of my lows, I consumed content from people telling me to get my life together. To lock back in. David Goggins became my alarm. StephIsCold videos were part of my everyday routine. Tony Robbins's inspiration pushed me to do better. And their words stung.

Every day, you have a choice to make. You can stay stuck or move forward. If you're not happy with where you are in life, it's time to change because if you complain, you stay the same. You know what you want, so it's time to confront what's really holding you back. These words would light a fire under me. A fire that grew every day I decided to chase after my goals in spite of my losses. Though I had the drive, my mental state was weak, which is why those flames were easily extinguished by the winds of envy.

My Instagram Reels were flooded with videos of this man who interviewed people on the street in wealthy areas from this page called The School of Hard Knockz. The interviewer is a persistent and driven man named James Dumoulin. James would open up with a line that'll be sure to get your attention. "Excuse me, sir. Have you ever been broke before?" or "Excuse me, ma'am, why did you choose your line of business?" These questions bring out the authenticity in a person as they reminisce about the times when success was an uncertainty. From the restaurant owner doing ten million dollars a year in revenue to the retired philanthropist who made $980 million dollars selling RVs, one thing was common throughout all of them. Their success was only as uncertain as they allowed themselves to believe. They willed themselves into believing that long nights of ramen noodles and Monster energy drinks were only temporary.

An origin story to tell when once their tuna sandwiches and Salisbury steak turned into lobster rolls and Ruth Chris. As I watched with my own cup of ramen in hand, I wanted to believe that I, too, was worthy of such an origin story. Envy, however, had other plans. It forced me to wear the shades tinted with contempt and self-doubt, never allowing me a moment to believe that I could attain the heights reached by those I was watching.

My reactions to others' successes actually gave me an accurate picture of how I saw myself and the world. I didn't think *I'd be there one day!* Part of me believed I would never achieve that future. I only had two options. I could either say, "I'm moving in the direction where I want to go," or "I'm powerless to change, and my life will remain permanently mediocre."

It's easy to get caught up in the timeline of someone who is way ahead of you...that's the thing about timelines, though. They are independent of each other and don't always follow a linear progression. Each timeline is different from the next, and there are infinite upon infinite timelines of people who were, are, and will be in your shoes. People who feel inadequate and shameful because they feel behind. Only to be made worse by those who SEEM like they are doing better than you online. There are so many ups and downs to a person's story we don't know about because we don't usually hear about the downs. People struggle way more than you know. You aren't as far behind as you think you are.

When I began celebrating my own wins instead of tying my worth to the peaks of others, the weight I carried started to lift. Once I found people who aligned with my vision, where we're allowed to share ideas and show unconditional support for our dreams, it allowed me to fall in love with the journey rather than be clouded by my impatience. My life, once shadowed by comparison, began to shine in the light of my own quiet victories. It took introspection. It took risks. ▶

Try to appreciate, and value, what's already in front of you

It took me understanding that I'd rather walk out of the battlefield scarred by my losses than untouched because I never tried.

If you only pay attention to others' successes, FOMO (fear of missing out) will fog up your view, sense of direction, and contribute to your brain rot. You can't see the ground below you to move forward. It's only when you let go of envy and comparison that you can see clearly. Dedicate all your energy into your own life, and your timeline will inevitably move. Focus on you until the focus *is* you. It's a matter of putting the work in, changing your mindset, and adjusting your focus. You are more than capable of creating this shift. Trust in your ability to build a life that reflects your true potential, because the trust you foster within yourself serves as the foundation for every goal you'll achieve and every dream you'll bring to life.

Escaping to mask what we perceive as a negative reality

We were the kids wishing we were the grownups, not realizing that *ICarly* Saturdays and early morning cartoons don't last forever. We were the middle schoolers and high schoolers who wanted to stay in summer '16, swearing up and down that "Controlla" and "One Dance" by Drake were the greatest songs of all time. Back then, our problems didn't go beyond our parents getting upset at us for telling them about our class project last minute and having them yell at us on the way to Michael's and Walmart for glue and a trifold poster board.

I look back at these times and cringe at parts of who I was. Young and corny. Then, I remember to give myself grace because I was just a kid. Usually, this is a statement used to minimize or discount a child's experience or absolve responsibility. But when I think back, I really was just a kid. A kid with complex ways of viewing the world. A kid who grew to understand that sunny days wouldn't be so special if it weren't for rain. A kid who emphasized deeply with the people around him. Though my emotional maturity wasn't nearly where it is now, I recognize that the feelings I carried as a child were just as complex and nuanced as the ones I carry now.

We all carry that same kid inside ourselves on our paths to maturity, and as we grow, our feelings mature. Middle school turns to junior high, and gone with it are the gentle anxieties of simpler days. The pressures of life start creeping in and force us to take our feelings in stride. Anxiety used to be from giving your crush a gift for Secret Santa. Now, it's about planning your life out before you're even eighteen. *You have time...but you don't.* Our feelings get more intense as we take up more responsibility and grow more of an understanding of the world.

This intensity only grows as life continues to hit you with everything, all the time, all at once. Going to college could look like working odd jobs to stay ahead of your loans and make ends meet, all while trying to balance a social life and good grades. If college wasn't your route of choice, then post-high school probably looks more of the same, without the cushion of a degree and external pressures to find a career. Growing into an adult means experiencing grief and trying to give yourself time to cherish the memories of the dearly departed. The stresses of life can easily manifest themselves into depression, anxiety, or any feeling that brings you sadness and unease.

Life is a grind we didn't sign up for. It's overwhelming, and rightfully so. This is one of the reasons why the things we once turned to for curiosity and fun slowly become escapes from a stressful reality. Late-night smoke sessions and Insomnia Cookie runs with your friends turn into: "I just have to deal with my boss for two more hours—there's a blunt waiting for me at home." PS5 Party Chat with the boys turns into: "Once I finish these last two paragraphs, Call of Duty has my name for the next ten hours." The mediums we once innocently enjoyed now feel like our only sense of relief.

In this case, relief is not resolution, and comfort is not clarity. You might think using your joint as a nightcap to take the edge off is harmless. Or maybe a quick scroll down TikTok to transition your mind from work to home feels like nothing compared to the grind you put in today. ▶

But as we both know, it never ends there. These vices, if left unchecked, become a poison disguised as routine. And bad routines harden into bad habits—habits that are easy to justify when life feels hard. This creates a negative feedback loop: the stresses of life push you toward false comforts, and those same comforts deepen the negative feelings you have toward your situation. Meanwhile, the real problem—your identity and purpose—remains buried underneath it all.

These vices wouldn't be so persistent in your life if you didn't have a fragile sense of purpose. When your identity is weak, your purpose follows suit, and you have no direction in doing the things you do. This, compounded with a boring routine, leads to brain rot. A negative feedback loop where you run back to your vices when things get tough. Even in the hardest moments, when life is letting its hands go, we all need something to look forward to—something to work toward.

During those long shifts working for what feels like pennies or during overnight study sessions powered by a can of Celsius, there has to be something deeper driving you. Something beyond just surviving. Beyond simply making ends meet. What is your reason why? Remember: your "why" isn't your purpose—it's the force that fuels it. And your purpose is intertwined with your identity. Somewhere along the chain, there's a broken link disrupting the balance.

When the chains are weak, you are weak. It's easier to fall into destructive habits when there's nothing pulling you forward. Without a clear sense of who you are or what you're meant to do, every day feels like a pointless means to an end—a relentless grind with no destination. I say this as someone who's been there. In the midst of my own trials and tribulations, I found my north star—the thing that kept me moving. I found it because I refused to stop searching.

I didn't find it when I was grinding at Dollar Tree for $400 bi-weekly checks, but I was looking.

I didn't find it when I blew my Pell Grant refund and went broke my freshman year of college buying PandaBuy Drip and Uber Eats, but I was getting closer.

It wasn't when I was going through terrible depressive periods in my sophomore and junior years, compounded with debt, falling grades, and confusion about where my life was headed, but I had an idea of what it was as I willed myself out of those tribulations. I drilled my "why" into my mind timelessly until it became a part of me.

Victory isn't getting to the end of the tunnel. It's crawling through the darkness. At times, I stopped crawling toward the light because the darkness was blinding enough, but I knew that as long as I kept moving, I was winning, even if my victories were silent. As you crawl, the tunnel gets brighter, but you'll notice you aren't getting closer to the end of the tunnel. You are creating your own light. A light that gets brighter every time you choose to keep crawling. My execution wasn't perfect—far from it— but every time I veered off course, my "why" brought me back. You can find yours too. The path might not be clear right now, but if you keep searching, you'll discover the reason that keeps you grounded, no matter what life throws at you.

Trauma

There are a million and one ways to describe Trauma. We often joke around with the term to describe a bad situation, like an exam way harder than it's supposed to be or seeing something on your timeline so deranged that it makes you want to rinse your eyes with bleach. It's so widely used that the word has lost its gravity. I've fallen victim to incorrectly using this term myself. I remember a time when my card declined at McDonalds when I tried to buy a McDouble. After trying a few times, a random high school kid in line said, "Third time's not the charm for you, unc. Give it up."

First of all, I didn't know being 21 was unc status. Secondly, as the cashiers were laughing, I remember thinking how traumatizing that situation was.

Now, looking back, hindsight tells me what I felt was embarrassment, not trauma. The word, as normalized as it became, holds serious weight to it and needs to be treated with the respect it deserves.

There are so many different types of trauma to just sum it up into one definition. If you were unfortunate enough to be in the vicinity of a grenade, C4, or gas explosion, you probably experienced blast trauma. If you've been exposed to extreme heat to the point where it burns your skin, that's burn trauma. Penetrating trauma is caused by anything that pierces your body, whether it be a gunshot wound or a stab wound.

But that's all physical. The trauma I speak of is more psychological in nature.

When people think about psychologically based trauma, minds immediately race to PTSD. They'll think of a grandparent telling their WWII stories. An auntie reliving the treacherous but transformative Civil Rights Era, who tells stories of marching with Dr. King, Malcolm X, and Duke Dennis. Even physical trauma can develop into psychological trauma after a period of time.

When I went to the Dominican Republic during my spring break, a buggy crashed during our excursion, leaving my friends and I seriously injured. It was concussions, broken bones, fractures, and memory loss all around. For a long time after that, seatbelt clicks and car engines would trigger a stress response in my body. You would've thought I served in Vietnam the way I ducked every time I heard a car exhaust pop. ▶

On a more serious note, there is another physical trauma that has a lasting effect psychologically. Victims of sexual assault and physical abuse exhibit signs of extreme mental duress. About 81% of sexual assault survivors exhibited significant PTSD symptoms one-week post-assault. After one month–the earliest point for a PTSD diagnosis—75% met the criteria for the disorder.[16]

These forms of trauma carry a gravity that cannot be overstated, and their complexities deserve the care and guidance of trained professionals.

Though PTSD is a common form of trauma, that generalization does a lot of harm in identifying types of trauma in your life. It is only a subset of the three different types of trauma- ACUTE, CHRONIC, AND COMPLEX. It's important to understand these types of trauma to understand where your experiences fall.

TYPE I trauma, also known as acute trauma, is a result of a single, isolated event that leaves a lasting imprint psychologically. Think of a singular jab that breaks your nose. These one-off instances can range in severity, which implies that recovery ranges as well.[17]

TYPE II trauma, also known as chronic trauma, stems from repeated or prolonged exposure to traumatic events. Instead of a jab, think of a barrage of the same punches over and over again. It's the weight of hearing the same hurtful words for years, the ache of waking up every day in an environment that drains you, or the silent damage inflicted by a cycle you can't seem to break.[17]

COMPLEX TRAUMA, on the other hand, digs even deeper. It's different types of traumatic events continuously inflicted onto you. Unlike a jab or a barrage of the same punches, think of a combination of hooks, uppercuts, and jabs repeatedly over time. Complex trauma is interpersonal in nature. An entanglement of betrayals, neglect, and harm that lingers long after the moments themselves pass. It weaves itself into identity, behavior, and relationships, leaving a person struggling to feel whole.[17]

Let's explore the three different types of psychological trauma through a series of short stories.

Type 1 Trauma (Acute Trauma)

Tylil is a Twitch streamer from New York. His rise to fame is largely due to his charisma and authenticity, but most importantly, his welcoming nature. Every stream is a vibe waiting to happen.

Though his fame has elevated him to new heights, he still has his part-time job at the local bodega. His humble roots keep him grounded in his ascent to fame.

After an 8-hour stream, thanking his Twitch Prime subs for donating gifts, he puts on his bodega cap and takes the dreaded one train to work, where he's going to be yelled at for forgetting to put ketchup on a chopped cheese. Every commute to work, a fan wants a picture, a girl wants his number, and a new streamer who happens to run into him on the train always asks for a collab. Being the inner city kid who found a way for himself and his people through entertainment, he's never one to think he's too good for a picture or a conversation with anyone who supports him.

One particular day, he gets approached by a fan. "Tylil, I love your streams. Can I get a picture?"

Now, Tylil isn't one to deny pictures, but the one train was running late this day, and he's on his second to last strike with the Ock before he's fired since he's been balancing streaming and working.

"Not today, man, I gotta get to work. But I got you next time."

The fan was disappointed. It was his only chance to take a picture with his idol. Instead of walking away, he says, "Nah, there won't be a next time."

To Tylil's surprise, the fan swings.

The haymaker was violent but sloppy. Like prime Mayweather, Tylil dodged, his reflexes sharp. After trading glances, his fan let him be and went his separate way.

Tylil went to work a little shaken up, as this was the first time he had personally experienced the negative aspects of fame.

Growing up in inner-city New York, violence is hardly a stranger. Your guard must be on ten walking down the street, waiting for the train, or interacting with any strangers in the city, and Tylil knew and practiced this day in and day out. As he climbed social ladders, and saw how far his welcoming self had taken him, his guard naturally lowered. ▶

The trail of first-time fame is hard to walk since the lessons you learn hit you hard. From then on, Tylil questioned his interactions with fans and thought his approach would open him up to more danger.

From then on, Tylil was on his guard every time he saw a fan. He could be approached by a fan with the purest intentions, and his mind would always go back to the man who swung at him.

On his commute to work, he now sits with his back facing away from the door to assess who comes in and who comes out. When an excited fan runs up with a Sharpie and a paper to sign, Tylil subconsciously keeps at least a two-foot distance before engaging. The paranoia doesn't consume his everyday life, but it affects his relationship with his fans. Tylil went to his friend Rakai, who's been an established streamer for years. He asked him for advice on how to navigate this life.

"It's not about shutting people out," his friend told him. "It's about setting boundaries and trusting your instincts. You're not betraying your fans by drawing that line."

Tylil started implementing small changes to protect himself without losing the warmth that made him beloved. He opened up about his experiences with his audience during a heartfelt stream, explaining why he had become a bit more reserved in public. His fans showed overwhelming support, appreciating his honesty and authenticity that drew his fans to him in the first place. He also took practical steps: setting up a PO box for fan mail, changing up his route to work every day, and scheduling meet-and-greets in protected environments.

The paranoia began to fade once he became comfortable with the boundaries he set. Tylil had never completely let his guard down since that day, but he was okay with that. He learned that his strength lay in balancing warmth with caution because the same fire that warms you up can burn you just as hard. The incident on the train became a reminder not of fear but of growth.

This is an example of Type I trauma, also known as acute trauma, which stems from a single, distressing event that leaves a lasting psychological impact. For Tylil, the incident was isolated, but its effects can be just as profound. Even with the weight of an isolated trauma, getting over it is possible. Tylil leaned on his friends and his introspection about his newfound fame to get him through it. The lingering effects of trauma don't have to define you—you can confront them and turn your experiences into a source of strength.

Type 2 Trauma (Chronic Trauma)

Mildred is a first-year student studying fashion design at the Fashion Institute of Technology (FIT). She always had an eye for putting together outfits and pushing the needle when it comes to contemporary clothing. A fashionista, so to speak, and everybody knew it.

FIT was Mildred's dream school ever since she saw Zendaya in her Maison Margiela Artisanal Dress at the Met Gala. A marvel for many eyes but a dream for hers. After school wouldn't be spent on the game or the courts but rather on sketches in her worn-out sketchbooks. She would draw until the graphite on her pencil wore down to whispers, soft and gentle. Growing up, she showed her mother many of her sketches. There was an instance where she showed her mom a Givenchy-inspired bright blue dress. Her mother said, "Who is this dress for? Papa Smurf?"

Her mother's jokes used to make Mildred laugh when she was just an elementary school kid with a dream. As she grew older and pursued her dream of becoming a Met Gala fashion designer, the jokes soon turned to endless criticism. Year after year, as Mildred told her mom she was planning on going to school for fashion design, she's hit with the same comments.

"Do you really think you should be pursuing fashion? Why not become an engineer?"

"How are you going to make money with such a low-paying job?"

As Mildred focused on her college applications, she tried to push her mother's words off as just yapping or meaning well with her intentions. Nonetheless, she pushed through.

It was no surprise to everyone but Mildred and her mother that she got accepted to the prestigious FIT. Her talent found its way to the right people. For a moment, ▶

Mildred pushed her imposter syndrome aside and celebrated her win with happy tears, closed her eyes, and imagined her work at the Met. Her vivid imagination was quickly shut down by the screams of her mother as she realized her daughter's pursuit of fashion acclaim was not a bluff.

Every day, Mildred tried not to let her dreams get washed away in her tears. Though everyone around her praised her talent, her mother's approval seemed impossible to attain. It's hard to believe in yourself when the ones closest to you shut down your dreams time and time again.

On move-in day, she tearfully moved in with the help of a friend, as her mother used her disappointment as the reason why she stayed home.

After endless icebreakers and syllabus instructions on her first day, she picked up a sketchbook and a pencil to complete her assignment. However, as she sketched this time,

Every day until her first day of school, Mildred was subjected to words from her mother that could pierce even the hardest diamonds.

"You think those little drawings you do are anything close to what they do in the Met?"

"These careers require talent and knowing people."

"When you graduate and you're broke, don't come crying home because I won't give you a dime to spare or a roof to live under."

the graphite didn't move smoothly. It felt heavier as if the pencil itself carried the weight of her doubts and fears. Her strokes were hesitant, her lines unsure. Each movement of her hand felt burdened by the echoes of her mother's voice, questioning her worth, her talent, and her dreams.

She cried herself to sleep during her fall semester as she tried to overcome the weight of her mother's words.

One day, she took a deep breath, trying to remind herself why she was here, why she had fought so hard to get to this moment. That evening, as she sat in her dorm wiping away her tears, she saw a flyer on the student portal about free on-campus counseling. She hesitated at first. Growing up, her family never talked about mental health—or even emotions, for that matter. Her mother would scoff at the idea, calling it "Gen Z BS," But something inside Mildred whispered that she needed help.

The next day, she found herself walking into the small counseling office. When the therapist, an elderly woman with warm eyes, asked why she was there, Mildred hesitated at first. But then, as if she couldn't help it, the words started spilling out. Tears flowed as she spoke about her mother, the doubts, the pressure, and the fear that maybe her dreams were out of reach.

The therapist listened without interrupting, then asked a question that stuck with Mildred: "Whose voice do you want to guide your life—yours or your mother's?"

For weeks, Mildred went back to therapy. She learned to untangle her mother's voice from her own, to recognize the difference between the outside voices of criticism and the inner voices of truth. The therapist gave her tools to rebuild her confidence, reminding her that self-worth was hers to own.

Slowly, she started to notice a change. She wasn't drawing to prove anything to her mother anymore. She was drawing because it made her happy, because reawakening fashion through the strokes of her pen was the one thing that had always made her feel alive. Her mother's words still lingered, but in time, they no longer had the same power to stop her.

This is a prime example of Type II trauma, also known as chronic trauma, which results from repeated exposure to distressing events like verbal/physical abuse, domestic violence, or long-term neglect. Unlike Type I, the incident isn't isolated. For Mildred, the constant barrage of criticism from her mother wasn't just a passing comment or a moment of frustration. It was years of accumulated scars that chipped away at her confidence and sense of self over time. Yet, as Mildred's story shows, even in the face of chronic trauma, growing is possible. It takes time, support, and a willingness to confront the pain, but the strength lies within you.

Complex Trauma

Noah grew up in a family where athletic excellence wasn't just encouraged—it was expected. His father was a former NFL player, and his mother, a decorated track athlete, never let him forget how "greatness runs in the blood." You couldn't step foot in his house without being blinded by gold displays, constant reminders of the family legacy Noah was supposed to carry forward.

But Noah wasn't like them. Though he was incredibly naturally gifted, he wasn't interested in filling in anyone's shoes but his own. While his brother was looking like prime Kyrie on the basketball court and his sister was flying down the track like Sha'Carri, Noah's peace lay in the shelves of Barnes and Noble, the stroke of his paintbrush on a canvas, composing his own music on the piano, and the Discord pings from his friends to hop on the game. He didn't love the weight rooms, the drills, or the commitment that came with sports practice. The days of mandatory practice that his parents subjected him to heightened his disdain for sports. His body felt out of place in cleats, his spirit unfulfilled on a field.

At school, Noah wasn't popular. His younger siblings, on the other hand, were treated like hometown celebrities because of their talent and their parents' acclaim. Noah spent his days pursuing his love for literature and drawing realistic portraits of his surroundings. The other kids bidded on him for being a square, calling him strange for not wanting to take sports seriously.

The gym class was the worst of it all. He had all the natural athletic prowess, but no desire to use it to its fullest. When the class ran track, he'd jog past his peers and steal first place. When it was flag football day, his arm could send a football to heaven and back. However, the students around him never failed to remind him of his untraditional path. "Your dad broke the all-time scoring record in college, and you want to spend your days being a fake Picasso?" someone hurled once in gym class. "All that natural talent for nothing. It's a damn shame." Noah pretended not to care, but every insult stung.

Home wasn't the sanctuary he was hoping for. His excessively competitive parents viewed his disinterest in sports as a personal failure. "What's wrong with you, Noah?" his father would snap. "You think life is about doodling and books? You want to be Basquiat? That won't get you anywhere."

His mother would add salt to the wound, saying things like, "I don't know where we went wrong with you."

Every day, Noah felt trapped. He couldn't meet his parents' expectations, and he couldn't fit in at school. He was alone.

As Noah got older and had more of a say, he opted out of the mandatory practices his parents put him through. The verbal abuse intensified throughout the years as a result. His father's voice became sharper, his criticisms more cutting.

"I don't know why my legacy means nothing to you." "Disappointment." "Your brother is more like the son I've always wanted."

Noah began to internalize their words. He questioned his worth and stopped showing his art displays. His piano keys started going untouched for weeks. He considered pursuing a sport just to make his parents proud, but the thought filled him with dread. ▶

Noah's peace lay in the stroke of his paintbrush on a canvas

He was college-bound, hoping to find a major that was in line with his interests. The years of verbal abuse and neglect had other plans for him, though. If his college social life was anything like his adolescence, he couldn't see himself getting through it. So, he made a choice that betrayed his every instinct. He applied to all D1 football programs and tried to pursue a career in sports.

Noah arrived at a Division 1 college on a football scholarship, wearing a uniform that was a reflection of everything he was not. The recruiters were excited, and his parents were overjoyed—Noah had the raw talent that coaches dream of. To everyone on the outside, it looked like he finally "came to his senses," stepping into the greatness that "ran in his blood." But inside, Noah felt like a prisoner in his own body.

Every practice, every drill, every brutal hit he took on the field felt like penance for not being "good enough" as himself. He pushed his body harder than ever, not out of love for the game but to silence his father's voice that echoed in his mind. *Disappointment. Your brother is more like the son I've always wanted.*

As the weeks turned into months, the fruits of his unwanted labor shone through his performance. He was on pace to break school records. His coach always praised his natural talent. Most importantly to Noah, his parents and peers looked to him with respect, something that had been missing his entire life. He had a social life, even if it meant hiding the real parts of him. For a moment, the respect he earned seemed to justify the betrayal of his true self—until he realized the cost was losing who he truly was.

In time, Noah began to unravel. His performance on the field was inconsistent. At times, he'd show flashes of brilliance, his natural talent shining through. But those showcases of brilliance and success were met with his empty feelings. At times, when the ball was in his hands, the weight of his parents' expectations and his own misery froze him. He forced a fire under his cleats to keep him going, but those flames quickly extinguished since his motivator wasn't sufficient gas for the flames.

Off the field, the friends who used to send Discord pings were silent now. His sketchbooks stayed untouched under his bed. When he wandered into bookstores, it was only to look—never to buy since practice and academics took up most of his time. The piano at the campus music hall would sing out to him, but Noah wouldn't utter a peep back. ▶

One evening, after a grueling practice, Noah sat alone in the locker room long after his teammates had left. The room was silent, but his father's voice filled the empty space.

"Disappointment."

Something inside Noah snapped. For the first time in his life, he admitted it to himself: he was miserable. The version of himself that made his parents proud was also the version he despised. Who he was to his college friends was only a front to avoid the ridicule he received his whole life. He grabbed his phone, stared at the messages he'd ignored from his old friends, and then called one of them.

"Bro... I don't think I can do this anymore. I'm losing myself," he whispered into the phone.

His friend's voice was steady. "Then don't. You've always been more than what they want you to be, Noah. You just forgot that."

That night, Noah walked into the fine arts building and stared at the piano that sang out to him time and time again. His heart trembled, unsure at first, but as his fingers touched the keys, something clicked. Stroke by stroke, the frustration and sadness he'd buried began to pour out of him, manifesting as musical notes of relief. For the first time in years, he felt like *himself.*

The next day, Noah walked into his coach's office and handed in his resignation from the football team. The decision wasn't met with understanding—his coach tried to convince him that he was throwing away a golden opportunity. He stood firm in his decision and understood that walking away would mean facing his insecurities head-on and a lifetime of finding himself again.

His parents were predictably furious. His father's anger shone through the phone; his mother's disappointment was more silent but no less heavy. "Always leave it up to Noah to disappoint." was the last thing he heard before they hung up.

The words hurt no less than the hundreds of times he heard them before. They lingered with an intentional type of pain. This time, though, his pain wasn't followed by betrayal but rather a declaration of his true self.

Noah began to rebuild himself. He switched his major to fine arts with a minor in journalism and started taking literature electives, immersing himself in the things that gave his life meaning. He worked part-time to make up for the scholarship he lost from resigning his D1 status, but with a smile on his face.

Over time, Noah unlearned all the negative habits that came with verbal abuse and emotional neglect. The persona he put on so people could like him was a habit so ingrained that living authentically was uncomfortable for some time. Eventually, he surrounded himself with people who embraced his habits, which gave him the confidence to live in his truth. He learned to forgive—not just his parents for forcing their expectations onto him, but himself for believing their words for so long. He couldn't change his family, but he could change how he lived.

For his senior capstone, Noah held his first art exhibition, featuring a series of paintings inspired by his life. There was a football left abandoned in a field, a cracked Heisman trophy gathering dust, and a boy playing a lit-up piano under the night sky, which represented the peace he found in dark times.

His parents didn't come to the exhibition, but his friends did. His old Discord crew, now adults with jobs and lives of their own, gathered around his work, proud of the boy who had finally become the man he always wanted to be. Noah stood there, surrounded by people who accepted him for *himself,* and felt something he hadn't felt in years: peace.

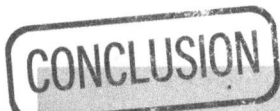

CONCLUSION

Trauma is complicated. You don't control where it leaves your scars, and you're forced to bear its consequences. Within the short stories, the consequences are evident in areas that show up in everyday life, such as family, social life, and career paths. Then, you have the deeper-rooted scars that alter your perception of reality, your perception of self, and how you interact with the world. Even the solutions aren't a clear-cut path. Mildred found resolution through therapy, while Tylil and Noah relied on the support system of friends. Like life, the outcomes may not be ideal, but peace doesn't come from perfect endings; it comes from embracing imperfections and moving forward anyway. Setting boundaries may mean parents pull away. Friends might drift as you learn to cope with your trauma. And that's okay. These are choices worth making for your own well-being.

These stories also reflect the two common themes that are reflected in a lot of traumatic issues: identity disruption and internalization.

Identity Disruption

As you may recall, your identity is who you are. It drives your purpose and strengthens your "why." When one of the chains is weak, the rest follows. Identity disruption can take many forms: it can mean a fracture in the identity you've already built, or it can be a derailment in the identity you're still trying to discover. There seems to be an overlap, but the key differences are timing, perception, and internal dialogue.

Fracturing what was already built

Fracturing the identity you've already built implies **loss**—the dismantling of what once felt solid. Identity building is not linear: some parts of yourself are more solidified than others. Confidence follows this same path. Once you reach a certain part of life, you grow an understanding of where your confidence shines and where it's deficient. A solid identity helps you grow the confidence you already have. When this confidence is diminished as a result of trauma, with it comes insecurities with your identity.

Take a star athlete whose confidence is mistaken for arrogance at times. Let's say this athlete suffers a career-ending injury at the prime of his career. With this injury comes doubt and insecurity about his future and the identity he's established. Their whole life was defined by excellence, which was backed up by their talent and hard work. Injury means hard work may not be enough to get back to star power. Grappling with the loss of something so integral to who you are can cause an identity crisis, which can manifest into a jaded perception of reality or an unclear sense of direction.

This type of identity disruption can also manifest through rejection. If you've been accepted in one space for your whole life but are an outcast the first time you explore other places, that rejection can create feelings of insecurity. If you've been broken up with in a situation that felt otherwise solid, that rejection, on top of heartbreak, can create an emotionally reserved shell of yourself, preventing you from opening up with future partners.

Derail the identity you're still trying to discover.

Derailing the identity you're trying to discover, on the other hand, is about **interruption**—the inability to fully step into who you want to become. Typically present in childhood, interruptions present themselves the first time you try to show an aspect of your identity. How it's received initially acts as feedback on whether you'll embrace it or reject it yourself. At times, you may even reject it before you give society a chance in order to protect yourself from criticisms you're falsely anticipating. This is called **anticipatory self-rejection**, which stems from rejection sensitivity, where you suppress parts of your identity to avoid anticipated criticism or judgment.[18] Trauma may be a cause for not knowing who you are because you might not have been given the space to explore it. That space that would've been used to develop yourself is instead occupied with doubts, insecurities, and misplaced steps in your pursuit of finding who you truly are. And instead of exploring it, you fall into brain rot tendencies that add nothing to your life.

Socially, this phenomenon can present itself when you're thrown into a new space for the first time. Growing up in a predominately Hispanic neighborhood as a black kid, I was both exposed to vast amounts of culture, but it was microcosm'd enough to where there was another world I wasn't exposed to. Navigating my identity early in my life wasn't a problem since I was ignorant of social and societal perceptions. It made it easy to make friends when everyone around me was also ignorant of racial and cultural constructs. That quickly went away, though, around second grade, when kids become more aware of the world, and their ignorance transforms from something once blissful into misguided prejudice. My peers were unintentionally racist at times, but the intention doesn't take away from the impact. As a result of navigating these complexities on my own, I created many faces and personas to protect myself and fit in. It seemed to work for a time, but it only lasted until my teenage years.

It wasn't until high school that these faces began to unravel. Early on, it was easy to mold myself to where I saw fit, and as a socialite, that seemed to be everywhere. That's the thing about molds, though. Sometimes, they don't harden the way you want them to. If you try to force a mold, it leaves cracks and dents. My cracks represented insecurities in my identity, made worse by trying to achieve universal acceptance. And as you mature, it's easier to spot whether a mold has been naturally formed or if it was forced.

Toward the end of high school, I noticed my personality becoming rejected in certain spaces. People became more honest about their feelings toward each other, and it was the first time I experienced some people outwardly expressing their dislike toward me. Though the number of people who expressed it were few in number, I still internalized it because I wasn't secure in myself.

When I graduated high school, I took the summer to reflect on myself and realized that people didn't necessarily reject who I was; they rejected who I was trying to be, which was an accumulation of different identities. Different faces I wore for different people. I grew to understand that I must live maskless and embrace the fact that sometimes, people won't like what's underneath. But that's okay. It's better to live in your truth and embrace what comes with it rather than be loved for who you're not.

Internalization

The first time you hear something nice about yourself, you tend to remember it for a long time. In elementary school, my crush told me I smelled really good. From then on, every time my dad gave me money, I made sure I bought a bottle of AXE deodorant to keep in my bag and spray every time she came around. Today, I have a literal arsenal of colognes and make sure never to step out of the house without a spray. You call it dramatic; I call it delusion.

On the flip side, negative words and experiences seem to linger longer than positive ones. The hotter the iron, the deeper the branding and negative words have a way of leaving deep scars. Those words or actions have a way of leaving a lasting imprint on us, guiding how we view ourselves and how we interact with the world.

This is internalization. Actively taking in and incorporating words or actions into your self-image so that you genuinely believe them to be true about yourself. You tend to make them a part of your inner belief system, which influences your self-perception, positively or negatively.

It doesn't discriminate between truth and falsehood. It doesn't ask if the compliment was genuine or if the criticism was fair. ▶

Internalization is like a plant that grows inside you, but if you haven't done the inner work to tend to it, you don't get to choose what it's watered with—praise or criticism, love or doubt. It all seeps into the roots and shapes what it becomes.

Those beliefs shape how you navigate the world. Kind words build your confidence, while harsh ones might come with insecurity and second-guessing.

No matter how our trauma manifests, one recurring result is the desire to escape it. This typically starts with an unhealthy outlet to avoid the pain of the relationship or situation. Then, it develops into brain rot through our vices.

Oftentimes, it's these very outlets (social media, weed) that prevent us from detaching from our trauma. Over time, our trauma starts to manifest in our vices. Weed becomes a false companion rather than a healer. However, social media, in particular, has transformed into something beyond intrusive. It has turned into an aggressor.

Identifying With The Aggressor

When I say social media has turned into an aggressor, I don't mean the type of aggressor that runs up on you holding a Glock with a switch. It's more subtle in nature, but the effects are more crude.

When I say aggressor, I'm speaking about the concept of "identifying with the aggressor," which originated in psychoanalytic theory and was first introduced by Hungarian psychoanalyst Sándor Ferenczi in 1932, later developed and refined by Anna Freud in her seminal 1936 work. It's a defense mechanism where someone unknowingly takes on the traits of the person or thing harming them.[19]

My high school best friend grew up in a verbally abusive single-parent household. Every day, she would hear how she was useless, a waste of space, and good for nothing. Anything she told her mother was met with criticism, leaving her feeling powerless and unworthy. In high school, she began to embody her mother's critical attitude, often gossiping about her classmates and using the same words her mother had used on her: good for nothing, useless, waste of space. Unconsciously, she adopted her mother's behavior as a way to gain control over her feelings of helplessness. She felt a fleeting sense of power and safety through this projection as a way to deflect attention away from her own insecurities. Her mother is the aggressor that she subconsciously identified with.

In addition to projecting the attitudes of your aggressor, there is an internalization of shame and blaming yourself for other people's actions and words. Your mind is constantly trying to regain control. In abusive environments, you may tell yourself that the abuse is your fault in order to gain control and feel like you can prevent it from happening. You're essentially molding yourself to the environment as a protective measure, not realizing that what you're internalizing is self-criticism and negative projections.

Around the time "identifying with the aggressor" was coined, Sigmund Freud, the creator of psychoanalysis, proposed that the mind is divided into three parts: the id, ego, and the superego. Though the theory is widely criticized and reformed today, understanding how the human mind was perceived back then helps put this concept into context.

The **id** is the part of your brain that acts on instinct and impulse. It is like the wild, impulsive child who says, "I want it now!" It doesn't think about rules or consequences; it just acts on instinct.

The **ego** is like the practical adult that helps to balance reality and the id's irrational choices. The **superego** is like the moral guardian, always focused on doing the "right" thing. It sets high standards and makes you feel guilty when you don't live up to them.[20]

The concept of "identifying with the aggressor" focuses on the ego. Anna Freud classified **identification with the aggressor** as one of the ego's defense mechanisms. The ego always tries to reduce fear by aligning with the source of the threat. It's not about empathy or admiration, but rather a protective measure to close the emotional gap between themselves and the threat, finding safety in familiarity.

Over time, the aggressors have evolved from abusive parents that ▶

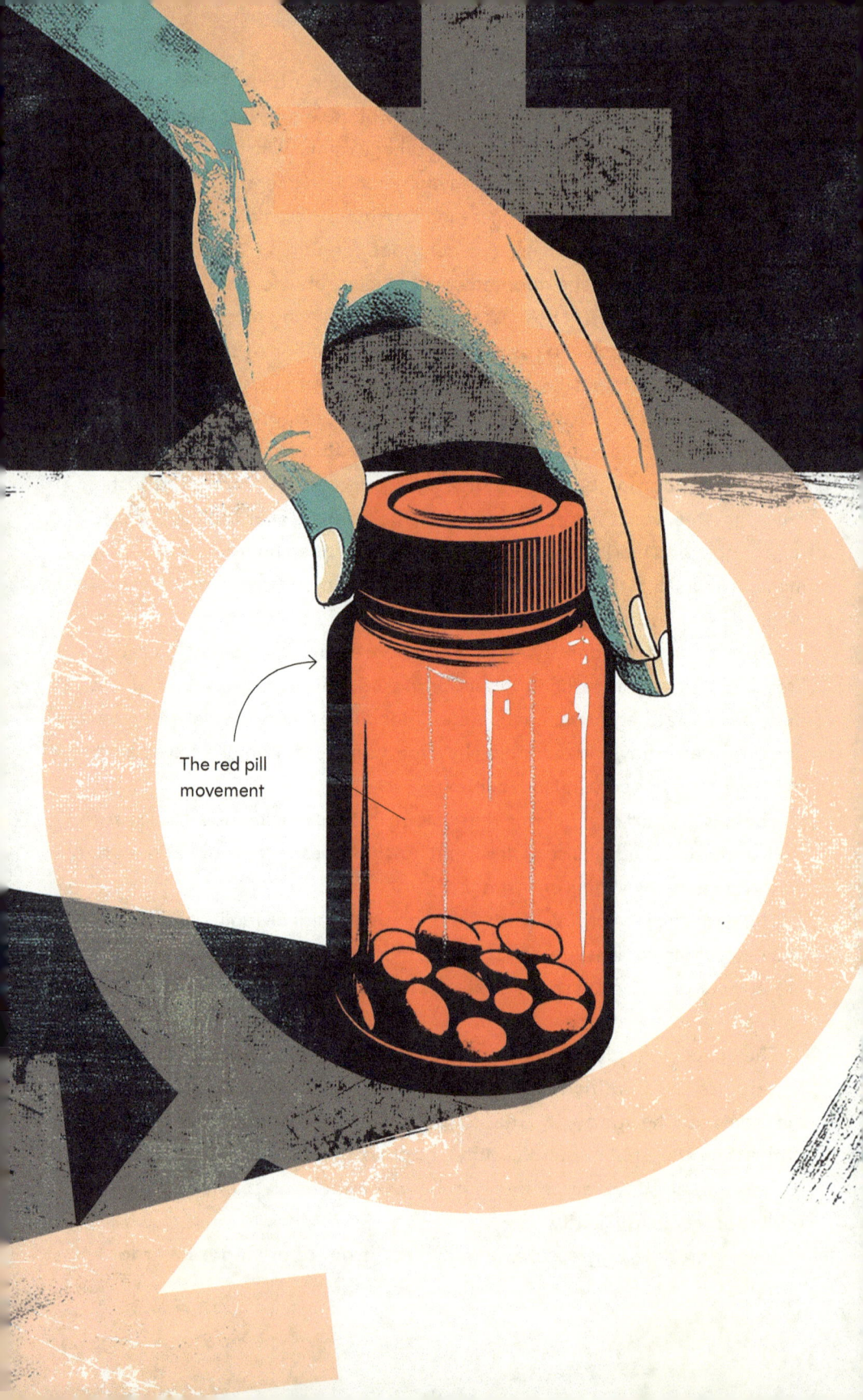

The red pill
movement

leave emotional scars, teachers who undermine their student's abilities, or bullies who shatter your self-image. They now take the form of the apps you can't seem to put down, the notifications you can't seem to ignore, and the vibrations that keep you hooked like fish on a line.

A symbolic aggressor with no face but endless ways to keep you traumatized. The aggressors are the influencers that parade their false wealth and tell you that you're nothing without money. The aggressors are the beauty influencers posting their bodies, telling you that you aren't snatched unless you're a 28 in the waist. The people who are rewarded for ignorance and shield themselves behind a screen.

How do people identify with these aggressors? Open any Twitter thread or any Instagram Reels comment, and all you'll see is a projection of insecurities. Lost young men who adopt a 'grind' mindset ONLY because the internet says you're less of a man if you're spending less than twelve hours a day on your craft. Women flying to Dr. Miami because their favorite celebrity has a body that's unattainable naturally. People that are quick to shame another person's mental health, financial status, or position in life to avoid the fact that they can't live up to the expectations imposed onto them by social media.

The red pill movement is the best example of "identifying with the aggressor" in the modern day. The red pill movement initially started as a way to fill a void of emotional support both young and older men were lacking. It was a manosphere with self-improvement tips, financial advice, and practical advice on dating. Eventually, it has morphed into extremist takes that tend to objectify women, overly glorify the grind, and lead young men astray. Because red pill spaces are so dominant online, younger men in need of guidance or older men traumatized by life's experiences gravitate toward these spaces in hopes of finding camaraderie. ▶

When I was 17, going through a late-teen crisis, it was hard trying to find my way on my own. It was peak pandemic times when a line outside a Sam's Club wrapped around a city block, and people were reselling Clorox Wipes like Supreme hoodies. I was losing friends left and right, had no idea what direction my life was going post-college, and felt terribly out of shape. This marked my beginning of the red pill.

At first, the content was not only refreshing, but educational. "How to gain muscle as a teen" or "How to approach the woman you like" was advice I didn't know I needed to hear. I watched them day in and day out. Since it was lockdown and I couldn't go to the gym, I started my workout journey with makeshift IKEA bags filled with thirty water bottles each. In the mornings, I'd put on my mask and run errands for my mom. At night, I'd stay up with my friends playing COD Mobile and finish it off with a workout while watching Red Pill YouTubers. Words could not describe how lost I felt at the time. I was just glad to have what I thought were voices of guidance and reason.

Over time, the red pill content morphed into something less guided and more exploitative. Alpha-male advice toward women centered around manipulative tactics. The grind was something to pursue at the cost of your health. I noticed some of these problematic takes, but brushed it off as a difference of opinion. After all, the red pill was forming me into the man I wanted to be.

I started putting their advice into practice, both good and bad. I kept my workout routine up to the point where when we went back to school in hybrid settings, people told me how ocky I got. It gassed my head and made me continue down this path. I had a false arrogance about me that I mistook for confidence. I was ghosting women to give off the illusion of availability. I was more reserved than I was supposed to be around people in order to stay in my "masculine frame." Every action I thought was building me into what the red pill says a man should be. I identified with the advice presented because, internally, I was very unsure about my identity.

Some people have epiphanies on their own. Others come from external interventions from people who care. My epiphany came from YouTubers by the name of Aba and Preach. It was the first time in my teen years that

I engaged with not only reasonable, but transformative advice online. Their takes on societal issues, approaching women, and building a life for yourself resonated with me in ways the red pill couldn't. When consuming all of that red pill content, I felt an inner disturbance that I always avoided. I kept telling myself not to get caught up in differences in opinions. Having Aba and Preach as my main source of content at that time taught me the value of patience, having a set of morals to abide by, and the true meaning of respect through their many anecdotes. It took real voices of reason to break the parts of me that kept identifying with red pill aggressors and projecting their behaviors in society. They helped me find my identity, which guided my purpose and my "why."

A lot of young people are unsure about their identities, their purpose, and their "why," which leads them down a path of identifying themselves with content that they don't know is inherently bad. Some aren't fortunate enough to find that voice of reason, and when some do, the negative content is already too ingrained in their psyche.

Inner work is a two-way street. The earlier you begin, the better off you'll be. The longer you delay, the more your vices will take hold. Understanding your trauma is a good start, but knowing isn't the same as healing. True growth comes from facing your trauma, rejecting its hold on your identity, and reclaiming your authentic self. Only then can you look your trauma in its eyes and put the middle finger where it hurts.

Self-Sabotage

Imagine you're an athlete—a rising star, even. You have a natural talent for your sport, one of the best at your school. You're not naïve, though. You know the starting roster positions are competitive at your school. There are leeches lurking in the shadows waiting to suck your success away from you and take your spot. You know what needs to be done. You lock in and grind. You eat right, you work out, and you sleep early, but you only do it a few days out of the month. It's enough to sustain you for a time, but you do this for only a couple of days. You're not really being consistent with your routine. Why would you need to, though? Your talent carries you far enough, and you still have your spot.

Fast forward. You miss some of the summer practices and take a lot of days off. Then comes the first meet, game, or scrimmage. You notice that others have picked up the pace from where they were last year, a pace you hadn't anticipated. Lobs here, dunks there, OBJ one-handed catches, sub 11' 100-meter times. That kid who was shooting enough bricks to build a house is now bouncing out of the gym. The sprinter who could never hang is now running Sha'Carri-level times. But you're still good, right? Well...you're slipping. *No, it was just a bad game for me.* Is it going to happen again? *I'm still talented, so no need to worry.*

But you don't change anything up. After that scrimmage, you feel the need to bounce back and perform like you used to. You get a short motivational boost to go to the gym and get back on a sleep schedule. You try it for a couple of days. *Okay, great. I'm on the right track.* But after those few days, it's back to the same. You only go 70%.

Then, as you play the second, the third, and the fourth game, you see yourself slipping spots. First turns into second. Sub 11 turns into upper 12. You're not catching the football like you used to.

At this point, what do you tell yourself?

"Damn, I'm washed."

"I lost myself."

Probably not. Instead, you might say: ▶

"Man, if I really locked in on my routine, nobody's even touching me in this sport."

"If I trained every day, I'd easily take that first-place spot."

"All I have to do is lock in for three weeks, and I'll be back to destroying everyone on the field."

This scenario, ladies and gentlemen, is one example of what we call self-sabotage/self-handicapping.

So, what exactly do these terms mean? The name says it all. Self-handicapping means you are actively or subconsciously putting obstacles in your way, preventing yourself from reaching your potential.[21] And the scary part about it is that most of the time, you don't even realize it's happening. You can exhibit this behavior daily and not realize it until years down the road.

While self-handicapping refers to missing and/or not capitalizing on opportunities, self-sabotage refers to missing out on better opportunities because of bad thought patterns or behaviors. Self-sabotage often leads to rifts or endings of relationships, typically rooted in fear of intimacy, childhood trauma, or trust issues. Thoughts like "She's too good for me" could lead to actions you consciously or subconsciously take (e.g., gaslighting, constant arguing) that lead to the end of the relationship.

Self-sabotage is more subconscious than conscious, though. We tend to make hasty, reactionary decisions toward people based on our past relationships, projecting our past onto people in the present. You can push partners, teammates, or classmates away or create conflict due to deeply ingrained fears of abandonment.

I mainly want to address self-handicapping concerning your goals and dreams. By the time you reach 25, you're most likely aware that *you* have to make the most of your life. Your mom can't go to that job interview. Your dad can't take your classes. Your brother can't drive you to school forever. From the ages of 16–25, you learn that you have to get what you want in life yourself.

Nobody is coming to save you. Whether it's getting a degree, going to a trade school, becoming a mechanic, working, performing for a sport or club-oriented organization, or interning, you have to make the life you want to live.

This epiphany hits you at some point when the safety net you grew up with starts to rip from the threads.

The cushion of a life you once had with Mom, Dad, siblings, and friends suddenly falls out from under you when you realize your life depends on you. You want to be successful? You have to go out there and get it yourself.

It's a tall task to ask a young person like you or me to figure out what we want to do with our lives. We apparently have to have it all figured out by 25. *We gotta do what now?* It's scary. It's a lot all at once. It's unknown. There's no guarantee. I'm dropping a fortune on something I may not love.

I still think about the amount of change that has happened in my own life. In a few years, I went from a teenager just kicking it with friends in a mic'd up Call Of Duty lobby too mature for kids' ears to becoming a full-grown adult asking where the time went. I look back at the Fortnite Season 1 days with teary eyes. I watched my sister go from binging Wattpad and Episode stories to navigating real-life chapters that don't always have happy endings. They're telling us we need to have a career in mind, a partner to marry, or a house to buy. **What? A Big Mac meal is $17. You're telling me this is the economy we're saving up for a house in?**

We have so much thrown at us. The social media, the content, the noise, and the distractions. And what do we gotta do? Somehow ignore all the BS and make a life of our own. And if life gets too hard, we gotta tell ourselves, "Ball up top," and keep it pushing. It's understandable that people self-handicap if they feel the cards they've been dealt are a bad hand.

It's easy to get lost in the maze of this transition period in our lives. Some people get lost along the way, seemingly giving up on everything they set out to do. They dropped out of school, quit their job, moved back in with their parents, stopped hanging around good friends, started smoking more, and spent hours at a time doom-scrolling. This is the greatest tragedy of life—seeing our dreams being sacrificed to our vices.

If this is you, you're not permanently lost. Nobody is. You can turn your life around, regardless of how many steps you've taken back. The more you've given up, the more work it will take, but you will get there regardless. Fall down 9 times, get up 10.

Self-Sabotage and Brain Rot

So, what do self-sabotage and self-handicapping have to do with brain rot? When our expectations of success become too heavy, we look to outlets to mitigate our stress. In this case, our generation turns to weed, social media content to cope. We find our sanctuary in them. Sometimes, the sanctuary we seek for comfort is the very thing quietly feeding our destruction.

This destruction affects the process of building your identity, which prevents you from finding your purpose and solidifying your "why." Identity building is not only about embracing the positives about yourself. **It's also about understanding the bad. The fear of chasing success because of your fear of failure.** The insecurities that have to be tackled through inner work.

When you start a goal, you feel a wave of initial enthusiasm, ready to make the necessary changes to succeed. That 3 a.m. motivation, if

you will. What happens next? You meet resistance. He's not too kind. It becomes difficult. You experience unforeseen circumstances. You start, but you don't finish. Giving in to the dopamine rush of beginning new projects and then quitting them shortly thereafter is a dangerous approach to productivity.

Say you want to create your own business. You begin watching YouTube videos on the topic. Good start. Over time, doom scrolling finds you, and you start soaking in information without action—a dangerous place to stay. The videos you watch make you feel accomplished, but once you start to act on all the knowledge you just acquired, you realize you'll need more than wishful thinking and dreams to make it past this phase. You realize your lack of discipline is heavier than you expected. The source of your action is spur-of-the-moment motivation. And that's all it is. A moment. Moments never last, which is why your goals never surface. Your dreams die when your action is absent, leaving only what could have been.

Quiet Quitting

Now, for some of you, it may be the "quiet quitting" that is getting the best of you. You haven't given up on school, maybe just on getting good grades. You haven't quit your job; just do the bare minimum. You haven't moved back home; you're just asking your parents for more money. You may still have good friends, but hang out with them less often.

This quiet quitting can affect your life in a very pronounced way over time. It's the decision to not go to sleep on time. To spend one less hour studying. To smoke after you said you wouldn't and get the munchies late at night. It's taking multiple days off at the gym. It's showing up a little later for class. It's not asking the teacher that question. It's ignoring texts or calls because you don't feel like responding to friends or family. It's more "home dates" with your girl because you don't feel like taking her out. It's turning the snooze on the alarm five times before finally getting up. It's this, it's that, little compromises that ultimately take you from a running pace to a jogging pace, to a walk, to nearly a standstill.

Self-handicapping, or as I like to call it, the "if I really tried" syndrome, will ultimately stop you from success. Barely scrape by the class with a C+ when you could've gotten an A if you "locked in" a little more. The business you half-started saw little to zero revenue but would've taken off if you put a little more time toward it. Failing to get a high score on the SAT you hardly studied for, but could've gotten a 1500 if you grinded just a week more. Choosing to apply to a bunch of safety schools instead of your dream school because you felt like deep down you couldn't get into an Ivy. "I would've done it, but I had x, y, and z happening against me." You start to blame the circumstances and events around you when the only thing you can control is yourself. You waste your life blaming everything else, but the real blame lies in the version of you that refuses to try.

Why do we do this?

Defense Mechanism, Fear, & Cognitive Dissonance

In short, self-handicapping is a defense mechanism rooted in fear, and if left unchecked, it can worsen your cognitive dissonance by creating a gap between your aspirations and your actions.

Self-handicapping is a defense mechanism to protect our self-esteem. We try to avoid any thoughts or ideas that will make us feel bad about ourselves. It's easier to say, "I could've done it if I really tried," than to say, "I didn't do it because I was lazy or selfish." We don't want to look at ourselves as the person responsible for our failures.[22] The more we defend ourselves against the truth, the more we see a paradox between two core ideas related to self-sabotage: "I want to succeed," and "I didn't try enough."

Success is innate. Ten thousand years ago, success was defined by a good winter harvest, sufficient hunting, and successfully increasing your means of survival. We've evolved to chase more subjective measures of success. Climbing the corporate ladder. Becoming an entrepreneur. Starting a successful auto shop that you can pass down to your future family. Becoming part of FaZe Clan. Success is tied to our self-worth, dreams, and identity. It's a path filled with uncertainty, but the upside beats a life of complacency. Most of you who chase success know this already. The "want" to succeed is already instilled in you. On the other hand, failure is a direct threat to our self-esteem. We fear failure because it attacks our self-esteem. We fear success because the road to achieve it seems so daunting, that we don't think it can be done. What happens then? Fear creates a protective persona. It lies to you with a familiar tone. It blocks out the truth because you're too afraid to confront it. It subconsciously tells you, "Don't put all your effort. What if you fail? You need an excuse to fall back on." This mental safety net protects your ego. It allows you to preserve the illusion that if you had given it your all, you would've succeeded. But in reality, you're holding yourself back from discovering what your full potential looks like.

These two conflicting ideas create a mental tug of war. Cognitive Dissonance. On one hand, you might believe in your ability and desire to succeed, no matter how daunting the journey may seem. On the other hand, you self-sabotage yourself and act in ways that undermine that success.

This dissonance manifests in four main ways:

1. **Rationalization:**

   Excuses Excuses Excuses. You become a book of justifications and rationalizations. ("I had too much going on," "It wasn't the right time," "I wasn't feeling my best.")

2. **Deflection:**

   You blame everyone else but yourself. ("The teacher didn't explain it well," "The system is rigged against me." "Fight the power!")

3. **Minimization:**

   To protect your ego, you downplay the importance of the goal. ("Eh, It wasn't that important anyway," "I didn't really want it.")

4. **Idealization:**

   You dream of a life you could be living. You create a mental image of how successful you *could* be if you really tried. Fear acts as a shield to help you avoid confronting your current reality.

This cognitive dissonance then turns into a cycle so damaging, it feels impossible to snap out of. The "What If" cycle." What if I sent him a message? I probably would've had a job by now." "What if I went to the gym? I would've been in Creed instead of Michael B Jordan." You keep your goals at arm's length and convince yourself that success is possible if you commit. But here's the kicker. You never do. You find everyone to blame but yourself.

But it was you. You gave up. It's okay to own it. You consciously put just half your efforts into a goal, and the proof is in the pudding. You believe failure isn't a reflection of you because you didn't fully try. These are difficult truths to confront.

CONCLUSION

What if you can confront your truths and live a life where you hold yourself accountable? What if your dreams don't have to die? Well, they don't. Your dreams are an extension of you. A manifestation of what you truly desire. You owe it to yourself to chase it relentlessly, failing in the process, but not letting those failures define you. Be proud of the scars you accumulate when chasing your dreams, as they'll always remind you of the journey once you've made it. On the other side of fear is either success or a stepping stone toward it.

How Can I Fix Me?

We are now entering the practical exercises portion of the book. You will fix your brain rot one exercise at a time. The series of exercises aims to accomplish two goals:

1. **Discover and recover your identity, purpose, and "why"**
2. **Proactively work on yourself and your goals each day**

Baby steps. It's all dependent on you and how much you want to change. Each section and exercise builds off of each other, so no shortcuts!

Completing the first section is the most important to your growth because it sets the foundation.

You can space out the exercises as much as you want (days, weeks, etc.), but I highly recommend one exercise a day.

Finding your identity, purpose, and "why" requires you to shift your perception of your reality and reorient your thinking to believe your life has meaning. That you are here for a reason. To do this, you first need self-awareness to recognize what's holding you back in the first place. This requires a willingness to confront uncomfortable truths. It means understanding that your worth isn't determined by the lives of others but by your own value and the choices you make each day. These exercises serve as a guide to help you get there.

Here are the exercises organized in chronological order:

Introspection (anecdotes/affirmations)
- Nothing Journal
- Brutally Exploring the Themes
- Tackling Your Addictive Behaviors
- Creating Your Mantra

Everyday Plan of Action (paradigm-shifting truths)
- Purpose,
- Your Identity,
- Your "Why"
- Crafting your Plan

The Blueprint
- Manifestation (pitfalls to avoid)
- Understanding the Peaks and Valleys
- The Validation Trap
- The Action Trap
- All or Nothing

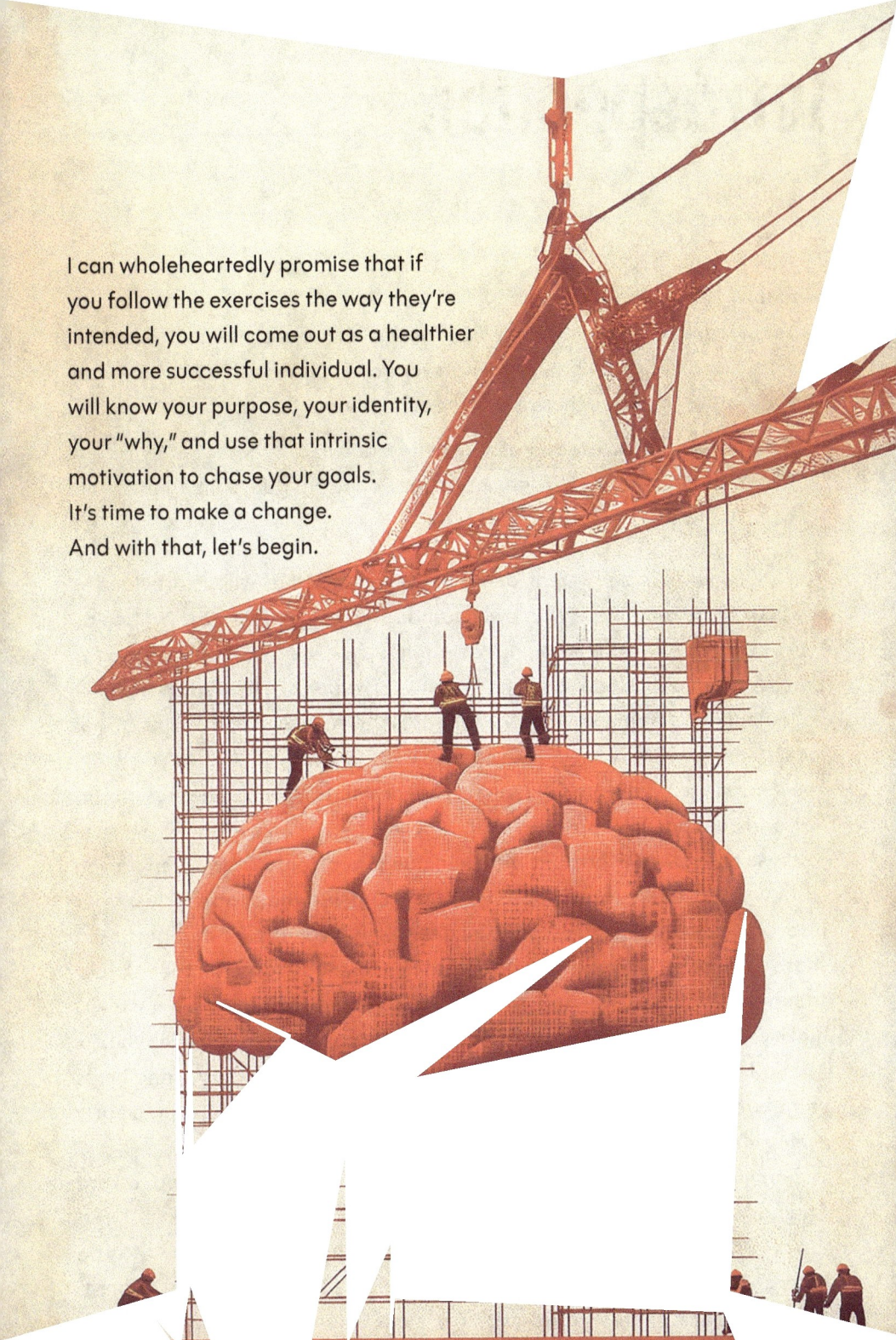

I can wholeheartedly promise that if you follow the exercises the way they're intended, you will come out as a healthier and more successful individual. You will know your purpose, your identity, your "why," and use that intrinsic motivation to chase your goals. It's time to make a change. And with that, let's begin.

Introspection

The Nothing Journal

I call this "The Nothing Journal."

Yes, it is exactly what it sounds like. There is no general theme or direction to it. It's just a copy and paste of whatever's on your mind. No rules on what you can write. However, there are some conditions to be met.

1 If it's a thought you're suppressing, write it down.

2 If it's a thought that brings anxiety, stress, or any negative emotions, write it down.

You MUST write in a physical journal. No excuses. Lines will be provided in the book if you don't have your own journal. The focused nature of writing by hand helps with mindfulness and racing thoughts. It's a great technique for processing emotions and reducing anxiety.[23] The point is, that you have to let your mind roam free and write the thoughts down as they come. This is your most authentic self. Without the shackles you place on yourself. As you write, you'll start to see your true self manifest on the pages. Your true desires, truths, lies, and passions will appear.

It will get you comfortable with being uncomfortable. How often do you sit down and really think about yourself? Outside the scope of just your insecurities, worries, and responsibilities? As you vomit your thoughts onto these pages, you'll have many opportunities to understand the root of your thoughts. The good, the bad, and the ugly. The epiphanies you'll have will make you realize that you might not know yourself as much as you think you do.

In addition, it'll get you in the habit of writing consistently. Writing helps stimulate your mind and will organize the "fog" blocking you from clearly seeing what's in front of you.

Forcing your mind out of your comfort zone is an important step toward finding your "why."

As you write, uncomfortable thoughts might arise. Maybe thoughts concerning depression, suicide, or low self-worth. Whatever it is, write it all down. Trust me when I say it's going to be difficult, but only journeys toward real change feel this way.

Take the emotions in stride and understand that this is helping you toward a better future. A future of growing, not healing. Healing implies going back to how you were before. Growing means embracing change and accepting that your past is a lesson, not a life sentence.

If getting started is difficult for you, I have five prompts that can help with the brainstorming process.

1. When was the last time you cried?

2. When do you feel truly safe and at peace?

3. What is something you wish you had done differently in your life?

4. What is a secret you could never tell anybody?

5. Do you feel like you're going to make it in life? Whatever making it means to you.

Exploring the Themes

Following the nothing journal, you will explore some of the themes you just wrote about. Is it a specific event or period in your life, a specific emotion, A person, a relationship? Write it down.

We are revisiting these themes through the lens of our big three (+identity). I want you to circle the words in each category that relate to what you wrote in your nothing journal (and what you feel in your day-to-day).

Exercises

ESCAPISM

Avoidance, Distraction, Fantasy, Isolation, Denial, Procrastination, Overindulgence, Withdrawal, Obsession, Numbing

TRAUMA

Fear, Shame, Helplessness, Flashbacks, Guilt, Anxiety, Suppression, Overwhelm, Resentment, Loss

SELF-SABOTAGE

Perfectionism, Overthinking, Self-doubt, Procrastination, Guilt, Neglect, Impulsivity, Comparison, Resistance, Self-criticism

IDENTITY

Confusion, Uncertainty, Belonging, Insecurity, Inconsistency, Adaptation, Validation, Self-esteem, Conflict, Pressure

How many in each did you circle

..../10

..../10

..../10

..../10

Based on your responses, I've created a criterion to assess where you are mentally and emotionally. The first one is:

Dominance in One Category

"Delulu"
- **Criteria:** You circled 0 words in each category
- **Description:** "Go back and do it again."

"Soul Searcher"
- **Criteria:** Circled a lot in Identity Only (6+)
- **Description:** You're unsure where to begin in your pursuit of finding yourself. There seems to be an inner conflict, preventing you from finding it. Whenever you get close, you're burdened with doubt.

"Batman"
- **Criteria:** Circled a lot in Escapism Only (6+)
- **Description:** You're burdened with pain. You tend to find an escape to avoid living in your reality, unsure about how to change it. Life seems to be a never ending source of problems.

"Self-Saboteur"
- **Criteria:** Circled a lot in Self-Sabotage Only (6+)
- **Description:** A master procrastinator. A notorious overthinker. Your fear of failure and mental fatigue is holding you back from your true potential. You have a notebook of excuses ready for when you're not where you want to be.

Trauma
- **Criteria:** Circled a lot in Trauma Only (6+)
- **Description:** A traumatized soul. A damaged heart. Life has beat you up with the hope that you stay down.

Dominance in Two Categories

"Woefully Diligent"

- **Criteria:** High in Trauma and Identity (6+ each)
- **Description:** You typically finish what needs to be done with a frown on your face, use your work or tasks as an escape from reality, or have the realization that you don't know yourself or what you're meant to do. Your confusion about who you are lies in the fact that your trauma takes up a lot of mental real estate.

"Insecuri-Tea"

- **Criteria:** High in Identity and Self-Sabotage (6+ each)
- **Description:** Your confusion about who you are lies less in traumatic experiences and more in your fear of failure or fear of the future. You don't have a clear idea of your purpose, and your procrastination continues to hold you back.

"Pain"

- **Criteria:** High in Trauma and Self-Sabotage (6+ each)
- **Description:** You might have somewhat of an idea of who you are and what you want to do in spite of what you've been through. Your traumatic experiences have a very strong hold on you. Because of it, action doesn't come easy. There is still some fear in pursuing what you know you should.

"Avoidant Hustler"

- **Criteria:** High in Escapism and Trauma (6+ each)
- **Description:** You feel you're always moving, but not toward anything meaningful. You dive into your means of escape instead of diving into your sense of self because it feels too heavy to deal with.

"Lost in the Clouds"

- **Criteria:** High in Escapism and Identity (6+ each)
- **Description:** It's less about the problems of back then, and more about the issues of right now. You spend more time avoiding life than embracing it, creating a cycle that's hard for you to break.

"Young Padawan"

- **Criteria**: High in Self-Sabotage and Escapism (6+ each)
- **Description**: From within, your greatest challenge arises, young one. You keep stopping yourself through procrastination and self-doubt. You have goals, but your patterns of behavior make it difficult to achieve them.

Balanced Across All Four

"Balance-iaga"

- **Criteria**: (3-5 each)
- **Description:** No single problem dominates more than the other. You might've had some traumatic life experiences that prevent you from acting toward your goals and finding yourself, but your problem lies more in execution than being heavily burdened emotionally.

Low Across All Four

"Low Life"

- **Criteria:** Less than 3 in each
- **Description:** You have problems, but they're not really *problems*. You're able to cope with your past and future relatively well.

Low in One, Moderate in Another, High in the Third

"If I Really Tried"

- **Criteria:** Low in Trauma, Moderate in Identity, High in Self-Sabotage
- **Description:** Trauma isn't guiding your life. You have somewhat of a sense of who you truly are, but procrastination is your enemy, and overthinking is the devil on your shoulder that prevents you from acting. There might be some underlying fear of where your life is headed. You might make excuses for why you're not where you want to be.

"The Owl (Who?)"

- **Criteria:** Low in Self-Sabotage, Moderate in Trauma, High in Identity
- **Description:** You're working on some internal issues, but you're often in a stage of confusion. You have no idea what you want to do, and since you haven't fully grown from those traumatic experiences, you don't yet have the space to explore it.

"The Great Pretender"

- **Criteria:** Low in Trauma, Moderate in Escapism, High in Identity
- **Description:** It seems like you have it all together, but escapism hides the cracks in your foundation. Your sense of self may be strong, but there's something you're running from.

"Lost in the Scroll"

- **Criteria:** Low in Identity, Moderate in Trauma, High in Escapism
- **Description:** You escape your reality more than confronting it. The act of avoiding life feels like a false comfort, preventing you from exploring your pain. You might have a stronger sense of self relative to others, but your vices got hands.

"Healing, But Not Growing"

- **Criteria:** Low in Identity, Moderate in Self-Sabotage, High in Trauma
- **Description:** Your traumatic experiences haven't hindered much of your soul-searching, but they have hurt you in other ways. You may have a solid idea of who you are, regardless of your trauma. Procrastination and fear still prevent you from attacking your purpose relentlessly. You haven't completely grown from what has hurt you.

"Chasing Shadows"

- **Criteria:** Low in Escapism, Moderate in Trauma, High in Identity
- **Description:** You're stuck in cycles that stop you from breaking through. Your identity feels strong in some areas, but trauma is that pest that lingers longer than it's supposed to.

"Burnt Out but Running"
- **Criteria:** Low in Self-Sabotage, Moderate in Escapism, High in Trauma
- **Description:** Your trauma dominates your life. You push forward more out of a need to escape than actual healing. Your pace is unsustainable, and the unresolved pain makes it hard to find joy in what you're working toward.

"One Step Forward, Two Back"
- **Criteria:** Low in Escapism, Moderate in Identity, High in Self-Sabotage
- **Description:** Procrastination and self-doubt are your sensei's. You know what you should be doing, but the fear of failure keeps pulling you back. That, along with trying to find yourself, no wonder your procrastination is so bad.

High in all Four

"Fight Back"

- **Criteria:** High in all 4 (7+)
- **Description:** Life has been a rollercoaster, to say the least.
  Feelings of depression, anxiety, and fear often fog your thoughts, making
  it hard for you to not only pursue your dreams but get through the day.
  You may know what hurt you and have no idea how to escape that hurt.
  Your mind blanks when trying to think of who you truly are.

The category I fall in is:

....

....

I think this is accurate/incorrect because:

....

....

I've been like this since childhood (PLEASE CIRCLE) ....**Yes / No**

When did it begin?

....

....

What caused it (or what do you think might have caused it)?

....

....

....

When I was writing the nothing journal, my most uncomfortable thought was:

....

....

And in my day-to-day, it comes up (PLEASE CIRCLE)
Not that often,
Often,
More than often
All the time

How does it affect you and your goals?

....

....

....

Explain if you think these thoughts are helping or hurting you:

....

....

....

Do I choose to engage in these thoughts/behaviors,
or are they intrusive/compulsive?

....

....

....

If I could change one thing about the way I think or act, it would be:

....

....

....

....

....

What is one memory that stands out as connected to these thoughts/behaviors?

....

....

....

....

What would life look like if this category didn't apply to me?

....

....

....

....

Who in my life might have influenced these thoughts or behaviors?

....

....

....

....

....

What are some small actions I could take to improve or address this?

....

....

....

....

....

If I knew someone who went through what I have, what would I tell them to help them through it?

....

....

....

....

....

Revisiting the Profiles

Are you a...? If so, follow the prompt that applies to you.. Pick One.

Dominance in One Category

Delulu

Think of a blank canvas and paint it with your thoughts. What would it look like? Reflect on whether this blankness feels freeing, overwhelming, or something else entirely. What could you paint on it if you had no fear or hesitation?

Soul Searcher

Spend 30 minutes answering the question, 'Who am I?' Start with what comes to mind first—roles, traits, values, or anything else—and dig deeper. Reflect on whether the way you see yourself aligns with how you think others perceive you. What parts of your identity feel true, and which ones feel uncertain or unresolved?

Batman

What is one thing you're running away from in your life right now? Describe what it would look like if you stopped running and faced it head-on. How might that change your reality?

Young Padawan

Think about a recent moment when you procrastinated or avoided doing something important. What thoughts and emotions came up for you at that moment? Reflect on how it might feel to overcome that resistance.

Trauma

Write about a moment when a past experience resurfaced in your thoughts unexpectedly. How did it affect you emotionally and physically? Reflect on how that experience shapes your reactions and relationships today. What would growing from that moment look like for you?

Dominance in Two Categories

Woefully Diligent

Reflect on a time when you used work or a task to distract yourself from an emotional truth. What were you trying to avoid, and how did it feel to bury that emotion? Consider what might happen if you allowed yourself to confront it.

Insecuri-Tea

Describe a situation where fear of failure or rejection held you back. What did you lose by not taking the risk? Reflect on what you might gain by letting go of that fear in the future.

Pain

Think about a time when you had a clear vision of what you wanted but couldn't act on it. What stopped you? Write about how that moment reflects your current relationship with your trauma and goals.

Avoidant Hustler

Think about a time when you felt like you were constantly moving but not progressing toward anything meaningful. What were you trying to escape? Reflect on what steps you might take to confront the issues you're avoiding and find a direction that feels fulfilling.

Lost in the Clouds

Describe a moment when you found yourself daydreaming about a different reality. What did that reality look like? Reflect on how much time you spend avoiding your current life versus actively working to improve it.

The Saboteur

Think about a goal or dream that excites you but feels out of reach. How have your habits or thought patterns held you back from pursuing it? Reflect on what it would take to overcome those obstacles and take the first step.

Balanced Across All Four

Balance-iaga

Consider the balance of challenges in your life right now. If one of these challenges were removed entirely, how would it change your day-to-day? Reflect on which challenge feels the most manageable to address first and why.

Low Across All Four

Low Life

Write about a moment in your life when everything felt manageable. What were you doing right, and how did it feel? Reflect on how you maintain that stability and whether there's more you want to explore or improve.

Low in One, Moderate in Another, High in the Third

If I Really Tried

Think about a goal you've always wanted to achieve but haven't fully pursued. What excuses or fears come up when you think about going after it? Reflect on what might happen if you gave yourself full permission to try.

The Owl (Who?)

Write about a time when you felt lost or unsure about your purpose. What external or internal factors contributed to that confusion? Reflect on how you might start to create space for self-discovery.

Healing, But Not Growing

Describe a part of your life where you've made progress but still feel stuck. What's holding you back from moving forward? Reflect on what growth might look like in that area.

Lost in the Scroll

Write about your go-to escape when life feels overwhelming. How does it make you feel in the moment versus afterward? Reflect on how that habit might be preventing you from addressing the real issues in your life.

Chasing Shadows

Describe a time when you felt like you were chasing a goal or dream but couldn't quite reach it. What external or internal factors made it feel unattainable? Reflect on how you might redirect your energy to a path that feels more authentic to you.

Burnt Out but Running

Think about a time when you kept pushing yourself despite feeling completely drained. What were you running toward—or away from? Reflect on how that experience impacted you and what boundaries you might set to protect your well-being.

One Step Forward, Two Back

Write about a time when you felt stuck in a cycle of making progress only to fall back into old habits. What triggers those setbacks? Reflect on what support or strategies might help you break the cycle.

The Great Pretender

Think about a time when you felt like you were putting on a front to maintain appearances. What were you hiding, and why? Reflect on how it might feel to live more authentically, even if it means showing vulnerability.

High in All Four

Fight Back

Life clearly got hands, but you swing harder. Take 30 minutes to write about everything that's troubling you—your fears, doubts, past experiences, and current struggles. Let it all out. Then, step back and try to make sense of it. What patterns do you notice? What emotions or beliefs keep resurfacing? Reflect on what feels within your control and what doesn't. Think about one small step you can take to start regaining a sense of balance as the storm passes?

Know that understanding precedes change.

This is in no way, shape, or form a substitute for therapy. Rather, the exercises provided serve as a guide you're creating to truly understand what drives your thought patterns.

(If you need a higher level of support, reach out to a school counselor, therapist, or psychiatrist for more intensive care and follow-up.)

Understanding your Addictive Behaviors

You learned that we engage in social media binging, weed addiction because of our underlying problems. Hopefully, the two exercises you completed above brought those problems to the surface and you now have an idea of what drives your behaviors.

This chapter will explore the types of behaviors you engage in and how they affect your life. There will be an exercise for each of the vices mentioned in previous chapters (weed, social media) as well as for vices not already mentioned.

Weed

Rare   Casual   Frequent   Everyday Smoker

3.5   8ths   Half   Zip   Ounce

3.5   8ths   Half   Zip   Ounce a month

Daily   Weekly   BiWeekly   Monthly   Yearly

Which Puts Me At... **$**   a month

And... **$**   a year

Tell the story of the first time you got high:

....

....

....

....

Tell the story of the most favorite time you got high:

If I go 1 day without smoking I feel:

....

....

....

....

If I go a week without smoking I feel:

....

....

....

....

If I go a month without smoking I feel:

....

....

....

....

How long was your longest T Break?

....

....

....

....

....

How did you feel after?

....

....

....

....

My favorite place to go when I get the munchies

....

....

....

....

My favorite friends to smoke with

....

....

....

....

....

....

My favorite thing to do while I'm smoking

....

....

....

....

....

....

Sativa   Indica   Hybrid

Why do you smoke? Be as vulnerable as possible

....

....

....

....

....

....

....

....

....

....

....

....

....

Relaxed	Calm	Euphoric	Chill	Productive
Mellow	Tranquil	Peaceful	Blissful	Content

The bad thing about smoking is it makes me feel (PLEASE CIRCLE):

Anxiety	Memory	Loss	Lazy
Depressed	Paranoid	Unmotivated	Impaired
Foggy	Addictive	Isolated	

Describe how

....

....

....

....

....

....

....

....

....

....

How does smoking affect your energy levels throughout the day?

....

....

....

....

How does smoking impact your focus and ability to complete tasks?
(Does it help you concentrate or lead to procrastination and distraction?)

....

....

....

....

How does smoking impact your sleep patterns?...

....

....

....

What does a smoke-free day look like to you?..

....

....

....

How does smoking affect your daily routine and productivity? (PLEASE CIRCLE):

Positively   **Negatively**   **No noticeable effect**

Describe how...
....

Are you a wake n baker? (PLEASE CIRCLE)

Yes   **No**

How does your smoking habit affect your relationships with family, friends, and colleagues? (PLEASE CIRCLE)

Positively   **Negatively**   **No noticeable effect**

Describe how...
....
....

Has anyone ever complained about your smoking? (PLEASE CIRCLE)

Yes   **No**

What do you tell yourself to justify smoking? Do you believe it?

....
....
....

Do you feel in control of your smoking habit? (PLEASE CIRCLE):

Always   **Sometimes**   **Rarely**   **Never**

Explain why ....

....

....

Future Goals...

....

Is smoking aligned with the version of yourself you want to be?
Why or why not?

....

....

....

....

If you could talk to your past self before you started smoking,
what would you say?

....

....

....

....

What has smoking given you? ....

....

....

....

....

What has smoking taken away from you? ....

....

....

....

Do you want to change your smoking habits? Explain why?

....

....

....

....

....

Social Media Screen Time Profile (fill in the blank)

What is your daily average screen time in a week?

Monday .... [ ] hours [ ] minutes

Tuesday .... [ ] hours [ ] minutes

Wednesday .... [ ] hours [ ] minutes

Thursday .... [ ] hours [ ] minutes

Friday .... [ ] hours [ ] minutes

Saturday .... [ ] hours [ ] minutes

Sunday .... [ ] hours [ ] minutes

TOTAL .... [ ] **hours** [ ] **minutes**

Go through your screen time and fill in the top 5 apps taking up the most of your time

From the fill in the blank exercise above, what is your daily average screen time in a week?

....h ....m

What are the top 5 apps taking up most of your time?

1. ....

2. ....

3. ....

4. ....

5. ....

What is your total weekly screen time

....h

Here's a breakdown of your yearly screentime based on your answers

1 hour a day:	365 hours a year	= 15 days a year
2 hours a day:	730 hours a year	= 30 days a year
3 hours a day:	1,095 hours a year	= 46 days a year
4 hours a day:	1,460 hours a year	= 61 days a year
5 hours a day:	1,825 hours a year	= 76 days a year
6 hours a day:	2,190 hours a year	= 91 days a year
7 hours a day:	2,555 hours a year	= 106 days a year
8 hours a day:	2,920 hours a year	= 122 days a year
9 hours a day:	3,285 hours a year	= 137 days a year
10 hours a day:	3,650 hours a year	= 152 days a year
11 hours a day:	4,015 hours a year	= 167 days a year
12 hours a day:	4,380 hours a year	= 183 days a year
13 hours a day:	4,745 hours a year	= 198 days a year
14 hours a day:	5,110 hours a year	= 213 days a year
15 hours a day:	5,475 hours a year	= 228 days a year
16 hours a day:	5,840 hours a year	= 244 days a year
17 hours a day:	6,205 hours a year	= 259 days a year
18 hours a day:	6,570 hours a year	= 274 days a year
19 hours a day:	6,935 hours a year	= 289 days a year
20 hours a day:	7,300 hours a year	= 305 days a year
21 hours a day:	7,665 hours a year	= 320 days a year
22 hours a day:	8,030 hours a year	= 335 days a year
23 hours a day:	8,395 hours a year	= 350 days a year

How many hours a year do you use your phone?

....

How many days a year do you use your phone?

....

Do you fall within the green, yellow, or red?

....

Do you feel like your screen time is too much?

....

Do you pick up your phone without even thinking about it? (PLEASE CIRCLE)

Yes   **No**

What was your favorite social media app as a kid/teen?
(Myspace,Vine,Insta,Kik...)

....

What did you love about social media when you first got it?

....

....

....

....

What did you hate about social media when you first got it?

....

....

....

....

....

....

When you reminice about old social media, what memories come to mind?

....

....

....

....

....

....

....

How do you feel about the content you consume on social media?

....

....

....

....

....

....

....

....

How do you feel like your social media of choice (Insta, Reddit, Twitter) has changed from when you first had it to now?

....

....

....

....

....

....

....

....

What do you think Social Media has turned into?

....

....

....

....

....

....

Why do you think Social Media has turned into what it has?

....

....

....

....

....

....

....

Do you think the fear of what other people think prevents people from posting what they want

....

....

....

....

....

....

....

Do you have that same fear?

....

....

....

....

....

....

....

Reflect on why you started using social media and how your reasons have evolved. Initial reason:

....

....

....

....

....

....

....

Current reason:

....

....

....

....

....

....

....

Do you feel in control of your social media usage?
Explain why:

....

....

....

....

....

....

....

How does social media impact your focus and productivity?

....

....

....

....

....

....

....

Do you use social media as an escape from reality (PLEASE CIRCLE)**:**

Yes   No   Sometimes

If yes, what are you escaping from?

....

....

....

....

....

....

Do you experience Fear of Missing Out (FOMO) when you see updates from friends, influencers, or celebrities on social media: (PLEASE CIRCLE)**:**

Yes   No   Sometimes

Describe a recent instance when you felt FOMO:

....

....

....

....

....

....

How often do you compare your life to others based on what you see on social media?

....

....

....

....

....

....

Do these comparisons make you feel like you are behind in life or not achieving enough?

....

....

....

....

....

....

....

Explain how these feelings affect your mood and self-esteem:

....

....

....

....

....

....

....

Do you feel that social media contributes to you feeling pressure to meet certain life milestones (e.g., career success, relationship status, travel experiences) because you see others achieving them? (PLEASE CIRCLE):

Yes   **No**   **Sometimes**

Which specific milestones or achievements make you feel the most pressured when you see them on social media?

....

....

....

....

....

....

How does your mind feel after a really long social media binge?

....

....

....

....

Why do you want to change your social media habits?

....

....

....

How long was your longest social media break? If you've taken one, how did you feel after? If you never taken a break, have you ever tried taking one?

....

....

....

What is one goal or skill you think you could have develop more if social media wasn't a distraction?

....

....

....

....

If you reduced your social media use, what would you spend that extra time doing?

....

....

....

....

....

How would your ideal future self use social media?

....

....

....

....

Why do you want to change your social media habits?

....

....

....

....

Create Your Mantra

There will be times in your life when you need to remind yourself who you are—that extra push in a time of need. When I was in my depressive rut, I looked back at videos I made with my friends when we were in the trenches, documenting where we were then and where we wanted to be. Those videos inspired this exercise. I realized I wanted something written to read when I needed that extra push.

This is where you create your own mantra. It can be written or recorded as a video. The only condition is that it has to be you talking to yourself. Think about a time when you were down and out and what words would have helped you get out of that place.

Speaking your goals into existence can be a powerful tool. It puts it out for the world to hear, to motivate you and hold you accountable, to acknowledge to yourself what you actually want. I make sure to speak my mantra out loud every time I read it, which I attached below as a guide and motivation. I named it "Behind in Life".

Behind in Life

When it's all said and done and the curtain closes, what will I have to show for myself? Seconds turn to hours, hours to days, and soon they all become a distant memory. Each passing year is a reminder that I'm not where I'm supposed to be.

I see the successes of the people around me. The people who made it out. The ones who created a life for themselves. Many of my friends seemed to figure it all out, and a part of me is happy they're blessed. However, envy quickly walks through that door—as much as I hate to admit it, it eats me up inside. Others' successes are bittersweet reminders that I'm nowhere near where I need to be.

The New Year's goals I so quickly contemplate fade into obscurity almost as soon as they appear. I can't stick to anything I try. It's not that I don't want to change, I do. I'm just my own worst enemy, holding myself back from everything I desire.

But it's okay. At least I'm trying to make something of myself. My past failures haunt me, but I understand that my past is only a lesson, not a life sentence. Everyone who's successful had to struggle at some point. It's just a phase. I'll get there someday. I'm sure of it.

What I'm going through now is the struggle before the success. The storm before the calm. The poor before the riches. My darkest hour has only sixty minutes. The pain I feel today is the strength I'll feel tomorrow. One day, I'll tell the story to a kid like me who will be in my shoes. I will tell them I was once down and out. I was once on the verge of giving up. They'll ask me, "How did you make it out? How did you make it to where you are today?"

I'll tell them I used to wait for the storm to pass before I realized I was strong enough to move the clouds. I waited for a chance before I realized I control the dice...

Yes, I wake up every day with the realization that my life isn't where it's supposed to be.

Nonetheless, every day I open my eyes, I already have two opportunities: a chance and a choice. A chance to succeed and a choice to put myself in the best possible position when the chance does arise. It's time I moved the clouds. It's time I controlled the dice.

Your Turn

....

....

....

....

....

....

....

....

....

....

....

....

....

....

....

....

....

....

....

....

....

....

....

....

CONCLUSION

You have now completed Introspection. As tedious as each of those exercises may have been, they were essential to understanding yourself. You first need awareness of how you cope with mental and emotional stress before you can ever make a change. Recognizing and acknowledging your bad habits is always the stepping stone toward relinquishing self-destructive behavior.

It's now time to move on to a new set of readings and exercises. The next section will empower you to explore your identity, reorient your life toward your goals, and establish a blueprint for success.

Everyday Plan of Action

Be True to Yourself

We've touched on the topic of purpose previously, but we're going to dig deeper into the concept as we complete some more practical exercises. But first, a couple of questions:

If somebody asked you to define your purpose in life, what would you say?

Maybe you've never had the freedom to make any of those decisions yourself. You've probably been told how to think, what to do, and who to be. You might have never even considered what your life would look like apart from somebody else's vision for your life. Maybe your parents imposed a career on you, or you were pushed in the direction that your teachers or counselors thought you should go. Maybe they praised you for your academic or athletic prowess. You're going to college to become a history teacher when you really should be majoring in business. You don't want to disappoint anybody, though. It's true that school systems reward routine over creative expression. A "get in line" experience, if you will. Maybe nothing was ever expected of you, so you don't travel too far into the future, imagining all the possibilities. Whatever the reason may be, knowing your purpose, your identity, and your "why" is vital to grow into the person you're supposed to be.

When I say the words "purpose," "identity," and your "why,'" what comes to mind? Let's go back to what they mean.

1 Purpose

What you were born to do, your intrinsic motivation to make a difference to the people around you. What do you want to gain more in this life than anything else. What skills you were born with and how do they help others.

2 Identity

Who you are/who you choose to be the moment you step outside of the house. Either your raw and unfiltered self or a persona you've created. Do you choose your true interests, desires, and upbringing, or the ones that are imposed on you by others? Your identity has to be in alignment with your purpose.

3 Your "why"

Simple, but why you do what you do. Who do you do it for? Why do you care so much about being the next influencer or going to trade school? Your "why" is the true motivation behind your goals and not the reasons society told you to have.

These definitions may be foreign concepts to you...at least on a personal level. You've likely ignored these three areas of your life because they've been imposed on you rather than explored by you. It's possible you're living someone else's life, restricted to what you were told to believe and what to pursue. It's like you're not allowed to live the true you. There always seems to be an opinion from someone else that overpowers your own.

Often, money and family are the decisive factors in choosing a career.

Let's look at the example of becoming a doctor. If you were to ask someone why they want to be a doctor, they'd likely answer something like:

"I love helping people!"

"I find it so fulfilling!"

"I want to have a positive impact on people's lives."

All of this may be true, but what did they leave out? Oh, yeah, the money factor, the family factor.

"Plastic surgeons make $500,000 a year, and I want a piece of that pie!"

"Both my parents are doctors. I felt like I had to be one, too, like I owe it to them."

"It's the only way to pay off these ridiculous college loans."

So why do we typically leave out motivational factors (like money) when discussing career choices? It might come across as shallow and disjointed, unnoble, selfish, and greedy. As much as we can lie to others, we can't lie to ourselves because deep down, we know the truth.

If you choose to become a doctor when it doesn't line up with your purpose, identity, and "why," you will always be at odds with yourself. You are just trying to lie to yourself, and you'll have the guilt and shame to prove it.

Another great example is those who want to venture into entrepreneurship. Perhaps you've already started a side hustle or have contemplated one for some time. Maybe it's because you are in a financial rough patch in your life, or you want to make it out of the trenches to support your family. Maybe you are already well off but want to make a name for yourself without daddy's money.

I don't doubt your intentions are pure, but there might be some discrepancies if you genuinely believe you're not in it for the money and the other benefits as well. Be truly honest with yourself about why you want to be an entrepreneur and evaluate what you tell others. There might be a disconnect.

You might say you have honorable intentions, like:

"I gotta make it out for the family. I need my mom to retire."

"Life is coming fast; I have to make something of myself quick."

"I don't like the idea of working for someone else."

Again, these may all be true. But have these reasons crossed your mind as well?

"I need a house in the hills with a Porsche GT3RS in the garage."

"I want to be able to fly to Trinidad & Tobago on the whim of a dime."

"I need to see at least 6 zeros in my Chase Bank."

"I want a rich lifestyle."

Attempting to hide your vanity—rather than embracing that it exists—will limit your choices and harm your ability to accurately assess your motivations. There's nothing wrong with admitting that a part of what motivates you is materialistic. Two motivations can be right at the same time. You can desire to help your mom retire while dreaming of that Porsche as well. It doesn't make you shallow. It makes you realistic.

There's nothing wrong with admitting that you want to make a lot of money. There's also nothing wrong with chasing a career with little money either.

We need to be realistic with both our desires and expectations. If you weighed the options, and pursued a career where success is statistically slim, but you're happy doing it, then you owe it to yourself to lean into that happiness rather than be affected by the rude remarks from people who don't respect your profession. At the end of the day, people will give you "guidance," but you're the only one that has to live with the consequences.

If you are tied to the shackles of other people's opinions, you will never be free until you truly understand yourself. Who are you outside of your family's pressure? Who are you outside of other people's expectations? You are *you*, and you alone.

Conflicts of identity often tie into conflicts of purpose. If you are always at odds with who you truly are, you will always be at odds with the choices

you make, tossed back and forth between the waves of what you want and what others want of you. Without a true and honest acknowledgment of your "why," you will never attack your goals. Your mind will reject your purpose and stay grounded in lies.

Before we venture into drafting our goals, we must first understand ourselves honestly. Without lies. Unfiltered. Then and only then can we create the foundation of identity to tackle our goals.

We'll now go through a couple of exercises to explore your identity, create your purpose, and understand your "why." We will venture from there to create goals and establish a plan to tackle them.

Identity (simplified)

It's best to leave your brain on autopilot and fill in the answers with the first thing that comes to your mind. This exercise is for you and you alone. No one else needs to hear or read this. Try to be as honest as possible without lying to yourself.

My name is ....

I'm from ....

I go to school/work at ....

"Me" vs Me
I tell people that my hobbies are ....

....

....

....

....

But sometimes I leave out ....

....

....

....

....

This exercise is for you and you alone

I like to listen to ....

....

....

....

But when my friends are out of the car, I like to put on

....

....

....

....

When people ask me my favorite shows, I like to watch

....

....

....

....

But my true favorite shows are actually

....

....

....

What's something you pretend to like but you actually don't:

....

....

....

....

....

Name a person you feel like you can be yourself around:

....

....

....

....

....

What about them makes you feel like you can be yourself?

....

....

....

....

....

What activities or hobbies bring you the most joy and fulfillment?
The activities that bring me the most joy are:

....

....

....and ....

....

Name a person you feel like you have to change yourself to be around:

....

....

....

....

What about them makes you on your guard, or change about yourself?

....

....

....

....

....

Tying Identity to Purpose.

My parents have always wanted me to be

....

....

....

....

....

But I've always wanted to be

....

....

....

....

....

I feel like their influence led to my decisions (PLEASE CIRCLE):..........................**Yes / No**

I played these sports..

....

....

....

....

My parents pushed me to play

....

....

....

....

When I went to school, or when it was time to choose a career, I pursued

....

....

....

....

But if I went down my true path, I probably would've chosen

....

....

....

....

My decision was my own (PLEASE CIRCLE)..**Yes / No**

If money was not a problem, and I could choose anything I want to be,
I would've been

....

....

....

....

....

....

....

If I was financially free and time wasn't an object, I would probably spend
most of my time doing

....

....

....

....

....

....

....

I feel like if I were to share my true desires, I'd be judged and ridiculed to an extent (PLEASE CIRCLE):..**Yes / No**

What I truly want to do is different from the path I took (PLEASE CIRCLE):..**Yes / No**

What I truly want to do is different from the path my friends took (PLEASE CIRCLE):..**Yes / No**

What I truly want to do is different from the path my parents wanted me to take (PLEASE CIRCLE):..**Yes / No**

My public persona and private desires are (aligned/divergent) because

....

....

....

....

....

....

....

....

....

....

Getting Deeper

What's one part of your identity that feels completely authentic to you and What's one part of your identity you feel was shaped more by others than by yourself?

If you grew up in a different environment, how do you think your identity might be different?

Have you ever done something that felt completely out of character for you? Why did you do it?

Do you feel pressure to conform to certain expectations from your culture or society? Why or why not?

What do you want people to remember about you?

....

....

....

....

....

....

....

....

....

....

Everyone has an opinion, and everyone has input, but not everybody has to live with the consequences of the advice they share to other people. There will sometimes be a disconnect between you and the people in your life once you truly find yourself and stay true to it. The disconnect is a good thing because not everyone knows what's best for you. You know yourself better than anyone else, so only you can determine actions that feel right when you do them. Now that you've assessed where you're at with your public versus private desires, we are going to draft your purpose and plan of action. We'll base it on what *you* want, not what *they* want.

Developing Your Purpose

Developing your purpose is intimately tied to your identity; everything you do is an extension of who you are. If you are loving, you will find ways to show that to friends and family. If you are diligent, you will excel at everything you do because you try your best. If you are consistent, you are a reliable person for your friends to reach out to. If you have a positive attitude, you see in others what they don't see in themselves. Each character trait you have will be reflected in your actions.

Your life's trajectory will be determined by how strongly you believe in yourself. That belief will reveal what you have to offer and help you develop a vision that best complements your skills and motivations. You have to see it, and vividly imagine your ideal life before it can ever become a reality. You don't know it yet, but a lack of a strong future vision is the reason why you fall back into destructive habits. If you take the time to think through your ideal life deeply with intention, those thoughts alone will drive you to work. The glimpses of it will ignite a light under you. Your purpose must be grounded in honesty and reflect your true desires. Your vision should be so strong that you won't allow yourself to betray the future you.

Let's go back to some of the questions from the identity exercise and look a little deeper at them. It's time to create your purpose and your concrete goals based on your answers. These are the goals you will commit to every day.

This section, "Your Purpose," centers around one question. You already answered it. Let's elaborate on it and write more as we develop our goals.

Again, what is your ideal life?

What is your ideal job or career? Fill in below:

In my ideal life, I work as..

....

....

....

and I have achieved..

....

....

....

In my ideal life, a typical day starts with...

....

....

....

includes...

....

....

....

and ends with..

....

....

....

In my ideal life, I live in in a..

....

....

....

surrounded by ....

....

....

....

What hobbies and interests do you pursue in your ideal life?
In my ideal life, I spend my free time

....

....

....

....

....

and ....

....

....

Who are the important people in your ideal life?
How do you spend time with them?

In my ideal life, I am surrounded by ....

....

....

....

and we spend time together doing ....

....

....

....

What core values and morals do you live by in your ideal life? How do these
values guide your actions and decisions? In my ideal life, my core values are

....

....

....

....

These values guide my actions by ....

....

....

....

How do you see yourself in your ideal life in terms of personal growth and character? In my ideal life, I am:

....

....

and ....

....

What impact do you want to have on the world?
What legacy do you wish to leave behind? ....

....

....

....

....

In my ideal life, I impact the world by...

....

....

and I want my legacy to be..

....

....

....

How far away do you feel you are from this ideal life?

....

....

....

....

Go back again and read your answers. When you're finished reviewing, take a moment to close your eyes. Then, imagine your ideal life. Picture the massive transformation of life even to the smallest detail. After doing this consistently, how does it make you feel? Good? Excited?

Is this life attainable for me?

(PLEASE CIRCLE)..**Yes / Absolutely**

If you closed your eyes and envisioned your dreams coming to life, you should have elicited some type of reaction: excitement, fear, optimism, anticipation, contentment, ease, amazement, or any emotion that inspires hope.

The hope for a better future should be stronger than the disappointment of where you're at right now. If your future vision is weaker than your current reality, you'll continue to fall into the same cycles you're stuck in.

If you were honest, what you wrote above is what *you* believe your life is supposed to be like—not your parents' or friends', but *your own*. ▶

Do you want to know what is one of the biggest regrets people have before they die? Living a life for someone else. Bronnie Ware, an author but former palliative care worker, wrote the book *Top Five Regrets of the Dying*. After working with chronically sick people for so long, there was one sentiment that she heard across the board: "I wish I'd had the courage to live a life true to myself, not the life others expected of me."[24] Instead, people live according to what society prescribes, what their family expects of them, and what their friends tell them, but not what they know deep in their hearts is right. They never chase their dreams or follow their intrinsic motivations, and they lose themselves in a job that never loves them back.

The sad reality is you only betray yourself if you throw away your dreams. Disappointing others is not fatal, but a purposeless life can kill your spirit early. It's not too late to chase your goals. It's not out of reach; you're just not stretching far enough.

A concrete vision is the foundation for a new life, no matter what your age. You could be a teenager, a young adult, or a middle-aged person experiencing an identity crisis. If you develop a solid vision of your future, you will get up every time, even on the days when your bed feels like it's laced with melatonin.

So, how does all this tie into your brain rot? How does this relate to changing your destructive habits? We all need a purpose bigger than ourselves. Something to take positive steps toward instead of the harmful habits rotting our brains. A vision encourages resilience in the face of adversity, guiding us through the treacherous walks of life.

Take, for example, the idea of parenthood and how it can dramatically change a person. The moment a parent first witnesses their child, their lives forever change. It's no longer just about "me." Everything a parent does will affect their child. How much they work to provide, how they interact with their child, how they nurture and show affection, how they protect, how they handle conflict, and how they use situations as learning opportunities. When a parent first realizes their child depends on them, they step up to the plate and work those 14-hour shifts to provide for their families. They wake up late at night with bags under their eyes to coddle their child and help them fall back asleep. It's sacrifice. It's change. It's transformation.

Much like parenthood, when we establish a greater purpose, we dedicate our lives to self-improvement and growth. We begin to snap out of the cycle of brain rot. Why? We now have a better use of our time. We become more aware of what's holding us back; we cut that out of our lives. We pursue hobbies, skills, or activities that will contribute to our future. You won't have time to smoke, scroll endlessly, or watch content because you won't allow yourself to. You're too busy going to the gym, staying late for class, showing up to work, or building your business from scratch. Your motivations change. You're breaking the negative thought cycles by building the future you were destined to create. You will bear fruit in the future if you find your identity, your purpose, and your "why" today.

It's cool that I have a plan for the future. But how about now? What can I do now to get there?

I'm glad you asked. What I had you do before was to show you how great your life can be and start the process of getting there. What I'm about to have you do is build out a plan that you can start working toward now to get you closer to where you want to be.

No matter what you want to accomplish, you will be taking it one month at a time. I understand how my generation operates. That initial motivation burst will blind you. That 3 a.m. adrenaline boost will have you feeling like Superman. You'll start working toward your goals like a man possessed. This'll go on until that motivation betrays you, leaving you with no other option to rely on your willpower or go back to your bad habits. If I had you focus your plans 3-6 months out, it's very likely that you'll start falling off course.

Hopefully, these vision/purpose exercises you did earlier allowed you to find a motivator other than the feeling you get from a YouTube video. However, what about the goals you want to pursue now? How about the plan I intend to have you build out? It's not like having a vision is an overnight fix for your procrastination.

Well, don't worry. In future chapters, I have methods that you can use tailored to our generation that will help you stay on track. For right now, though, I intend to have you build out your plan a month at a time. This will do two things. First, it makes you appreciate your smaller wins more immediately. Second, it gives you more of a realistic timeframe for getting things done.

Now, let's draft your plan. First, I will give you an example of how to complete it, and then you can begin your own.

Crafting your Plan

Crafting your plan will be simple and achievable. There are a million and one templates you can use to craft your plan, but none account for how cooked your attention span is and how underdeveloped your discipline is. This template is called 12 Steps, 12 Months, 1 Year.

Example:

My Biggest Goal For the Year (should tie into your vision)

Start a Clothing Brand

12 Steps, 12 Months, 1 Year

If it's a goal worth achieving, and a year-long goal at that, there will be at least 12 steps/action items you can write down, one for each month. The idea here is that each step won't take you a month to finish. Once you finish that one step, you can use that momentum to carry yourself into the next one. Every extra step you accomplish in a month pushes your timeline up. Let me show you what I mean.

Let's use creating a clothing brand as an example. We are the generation of innovators and creatives. I've had a lot of friends pursue this avenue, but not know where to start. Or, they'll begin, and lose motivation along the way because of how daunting it seems. This plan accounts for all of that.

Here's the sample plan as follows.

MONTHS	ACTION ITEMS FOR THE MONTH
Month 1: Research and Education	Learn from established brands, familiarize yourself with design, production, and marketing, and start by watching YouTube videos and reading articles about starting a clothing firm.
Month 2: Design Creation	Put that pen to paper (or Goodnotes). Create and improve your hoodie designs. Use design tools or software to produce prototypes of your concepts. Pay attention to your logos, color palettes, and brand identity.
Month 3: Supplier Research	Look into possible suppliers on Alibaba or other production sites. Speak with suppliers to find out about costs, sampling, and how much you need to order at minimum. Once you find one, make sure to create a good relationship with them.
Month 4: Sampling and Prototyping	Place sample orders for your hoodies with the vendors you've narrowed down. Do your own quality checks. Make any necessary modifications.
Month 5: Branding and Packaging Design	Design the packaging, tagline, and logo for your brand. What do you want people to associate your clothes with?
Month 6: Website and E-commerce Setup	Create your website and open an online store on a platform like Squarespace, Wix, or Shopify. Make sure your website is one of one and has your personal touches added to it.
Month 7: Social Media Strategy	Create a social media presence on sites like Pinterest, Instagram, and TikTok. Make a schedule for your posts' content and begin creating buzz.
Month 8: Sample Testing and Feedback	For feedback, send samples to friends, influencers (not QUAN), or local communities. Make any last-minute changes to your product using this information before it is mass-produced.
Month 9: Pre-launch Marketing	To create anticipation, start a pre-launch promotion and use early access incentives, exclusive discounts, or email sign-ups to generate excitement for your brand's launch.
Month 10: Production and Inventory Management	After completing your final designs and quality checks, place your first bulk purchase with the supplier. Organize your fulfillment and keep track of your supplies by setting up inventory management.

▶

Month 11: Launch Day	It's the MF day. Introduce your brand and open for business. Carry out your marketing strategy, arrange in-person or virtual launch events, and interact with your audience on social media.
Month 12: Post-launch Strategy and Growth	Examine how well your launch went by examining sales information, client comments, and social media activity. You should tweak this by expanding your brand, launching new goods, and improving your advertising.

Now, let's say the action items you set for yourself in Month 1 only took 10 days to complete—and by complete, I mean done thoroughly and executed well. You can then move on to the action items for Month 2. If you manage to finish Month 2's tasks within the first month (which is likely, as the initial steps often go quickly), you've just pushed your timeline ahead by a month. Instead of reaching your goal in 12 months, you're now on track to achieve it in 11. However, you don't have to move on to the next action item if you complete the one you assigned to yourself that month. The only condition is that at the beginning of the next month, you must get started on that month's action item. So, if it's January 1st, and you complete your action items for that month by January 10th, it's your choice whether you want to begin February's action items right away or wait until February 1st to begin.

When creating your plan, it's important to ensure that each step builds logically on the one before it. For example, design creation should come after research since you need a solid foundation of knowledge before proceeding. Similarly, supplier research should only come after your designs are finalized.

Why is this structure designed with our generation in mind? Because it accounts for the realities we face while striving for self-improvement. I'm giving you a month to complete action items that should only take half that time if that. Why? Because as you work toward your goals, life happens, and sometimes, old habits resurface. You won't be a productive machine right away. The extra time is built-in as a cushion, allowing for setbacks, distractions, or moments where you might slip back into your old ways. This structure is about progress, not perfection.

Your turn. It's now time to build your plan of action.

My Biggest Goal For the Year **12 Steps, 12 Months, 1 Year**

MONTHS	ACTION ITEMS FOR THE MONTH
Month 1:	
Month 2:	
Month 3:	
Month 4:	
Month 5:	
Month 6:	
Month 7:	
Month 8:	
Month 9:	
Month 10:	
Month 11:	
Month 12	
Start Date	End Date

Good on you for creating your plan of action. This was an important chapter in establishing your plan for the future. You will refer back to this a lot as the year progresses.

Now, you have a plan. It's time to talk about your "why."

Finding your "Why."

We've discussed finding your "why" previously in other exercises, and it may sound like another word for "purpose." So, why talk about the same things twice?

Well, you're going to learn that your "why" has some notable differences from your "purpose." Purpose is a broader concept, looking at what you're passionate about from a bird's eye view. Your why is more specific, looking at exactly why you want to do it and the reasons behind it. I mention it separately because I want you to create your vision down to the smallest details.

If you've spent any amount of time lying in bed, not able to fall asleep, and spamming YouTube videos trying to find that 3 a.m. motivation, maybe you were up pondering these questions:

Why am I here? Why do I do what I do? Why do I exist?

Pretty big existential questions, but we're going to look at the concept on a deeper level. Your "why" is *your* why. It's not the "why" you think you have to share to sound humble or down to earth.

It's not the "why" you manufactured to spare yourself from your family's backlash. It's your personal motivator. It's what keeps you going.

For some, their sole motivator is possession-based, to acquire "things," e.g., houses in the hills, yachts in the Caribbean, an audemars piguet for the wrist so you can hit the *Shedeur,* and the list goes on. I am not here to lecture you to change it (even if I believe your "why" should be rooted in something stronger). Whatever your motivation is, you have to remain strong in your "why." You must embrace where it's truly rooted from.

Allow me now to give an example of my unfiltered "why" so you have an idea of how to structure yours.

For the longest time, I wanted to be a doctor. I believed helping people was my calling in life. I thought I had my plan all figured out. Four years undergrad at Johns Hopkins, Med School at NYU. Residency at Harlem Hospital. I carried on with this plan all the way till 2020 when the COVID-19 pandemic hit. I was then met by an unforeseen reality. COVID hit service providers hard, and my dad was a taxi driver in New York. You can guess what that meant when it came to business. I was shown my family's financial situation, and I had an unfiltered conversation with my mom about it that changed the trajectory of my life.

My family did their best to hide it from me because a kid doesn't need to know these things, right? It's all about dreaming big and going wherever your heart desires. Well, not every time. After that conversation, I suddenly grew up, understanding every financial decision I made could have a major effect on others. I knew I had to make an ideal future that also contributed to my family. Although they never pressured me toward a career and supported my aspirations, I took it upon myself to change my trajectory. I switched my major to business. It was time to make money, and fast, for those around me.

The most common questions for a college student are, "What's your major?" and "Why'd you choose it?" To be honest, I had a lot of half-truths ready to answer with. Answers like:

"The world is a massive series of business ventures. I want to make a difference in people's lives using the money I make."

"I'd like to know that my decisions have an impact on the world."

Both answers are true, to an extent. I did eventually grow to enjoy business as a major and found a love for entrepreneurship, but my mind was set on making it out. Putting my parents and siblings in better positions.

The more I explored the traditional corporate business world through internships, networking, and conferences, the more I realized that a part of me was not entirely aligned with that world for a long-term career. However, I stuck it out because I knew my goal.

Honestly speaking, my interests changed as I matured and found myself in college. It's true that I wanted to become a doctor to help people. And part of me still held onto that dream as I thought about my life past a certain age. But over the course of my undergrad, I realized the investment of my time was too much for me to commit to. Four years undergrad. Then med school. Then residency. Then begin working post-30. There was a time in my life when I was okay with it. Actually, I was excited when I thought about it. Over time, that excitement dwindled the more I explored the business world. I used to think my motivation to switch majors to business was only because I wanted to make it out for those around me, my family. In reality, I had other motivators I suppressed because I felt like it made my reasoning (and, by extension, *me*) shallow.

Then I asked myself which aspects of business I *did* like and decided to dig deeper. I kept asking myself questions about what I truly desired, and years of trial and error led me to the raw and unfiltered truth.

The truth is, I'm motivated by financial freedom—true financial freedom, the freedom that entrepreneurship brings, and the idea of not answering to anyone.

Financial freedom puts you in charge of your time and decisions, allowing you to invest in what you desire most. You can, almost impulsively, decide to take different routes or ventures at the drop of a dime, lifted from the weights of financial struggle.

When I initially decided to pursue a major in business, I closed my eyes and imagined the bright future ahead of me. I saw the joy in my parents' eyes; they can enjoy the life that's ahead of them. I imagined sending my grandpa a check to renovate his house, giving my friends money to invest in their businesses so we could grow together, and improving the educational landscape abroad in Senegal. ▶

When I thought about it more deeply, I was also excited to get time back and choose my hours with the flexibility financial freedom provides. No more 60–80 hour workweeks with two weeks of vacation here and there. No, I get to work whenever the hell I want to work, and from anywhere in the world. I can become a motivational speaker and inspire people on how to better their lives. I can inspire others to take ownership of their lives and control their destiny. I can show those I grew up with what's possible when you decide to take ownership of your life. Growing up where I did, many of my peers felt limited by their environment. I want to be that example for the ones who want better for themselves but don't know how to achieve it. "If he can do it, I can do it too." Inspiring hope in others is my life's calling. The possibilities are endless when financial burdens don't exist in your life.

Financial freedom is my "why," but it's not my *only* why. I still imagine traveling the world, buying a nice house, driving a Porsche Taycan, and building out my closet with nice fits, just as I am motivated to better myself, take care of the family, and inspire the people I came up with. These whys do not have to be at odds with each other. My ideal life encompasses all of the above.

I believe my "why" is a combination of humility and selfless character mixed in with some vanity sprinkled on top. I've learned over time that it's okay to be a little selfish when envisioning your ideal life.

It took me a while to understand why I do what I do, the reasons I relentlessly attack my goals. My motivations are a mix of selfless and selfish factors, and it would be unfair to suppress the parts of myself that are vain in nature just to hide my selfishness. I want to love and respect other people, but not please them. Why? People pleasing never ends. But honesty? It always wins in the end.

When you draft your why, you have to be truly honest. What drives you?

Finding your "Why"

What do you tell people is the reason for wanting to achieve your goals?

I tell others I want to achieve my goals because:

....

....

Reflect on the emotional roots of your motivations. What past experiences or feelings have shaped your "why"?

My motivations are rooted in experiences such as...

....

because ....

What material possessions or achievements motivate you, and why?

Material motivations include

....

because ....

What non-material achievements motivate you, and why?

Non-material motivations include

....

because ....

How do your loved ones influence your motivations?

My loved ones influence my motivations by...

....

....

For whom are you trying to achieve your goals, besides yourself?
I am trying to achieve my goals for

....

because ....

**If those people were no longer in your life,
how would your goals change, if at all?**..

....

**How do your selfless motivations blend with your selfish or vain
motivations?**
My selfless motivations include..

My selfish or vain motivations include..

These motivations blend by..

What is the most honest and unfiltered reason you pursue your goals?
The most honest reason I pursue my goals is

....

....

How do you see your "why" changing as you grow?........................

....

Will you learn to be okay if other people reject your "why"?

....

....

In the practical exercise section thus far, you have explored your **identity**, which has determined your **purpose.** Now, you have the reason **why** you should attack your purpose.

Hopefully, you've been able to embark on a journey of mental exploration, gaining insight as to who you are, what you're good at, and why you act on those skills and attributes. By now, you should have a concrete example of where you see yourself in life.

The question is, how are you going to stick to it? What are you going to do each day to achieve your goals at the one-month, two-month, one-year mark, and five years down the road? *I created a plan earlier. How will I stick to the plan I created? How will I make sure I'm in control of my vices? What can I do about my lack of discipline? How can I decide to eliminate my addiction to weed, social media, and content?*

Don't worry, I won't leave you hanging. The next chapter will shed light on the solution to your everyday struggles. I call the next section the blueprint. It's the practical steps to establishing discipline in your life and giving up negative coping tools. Let's begin.

The Blueprint

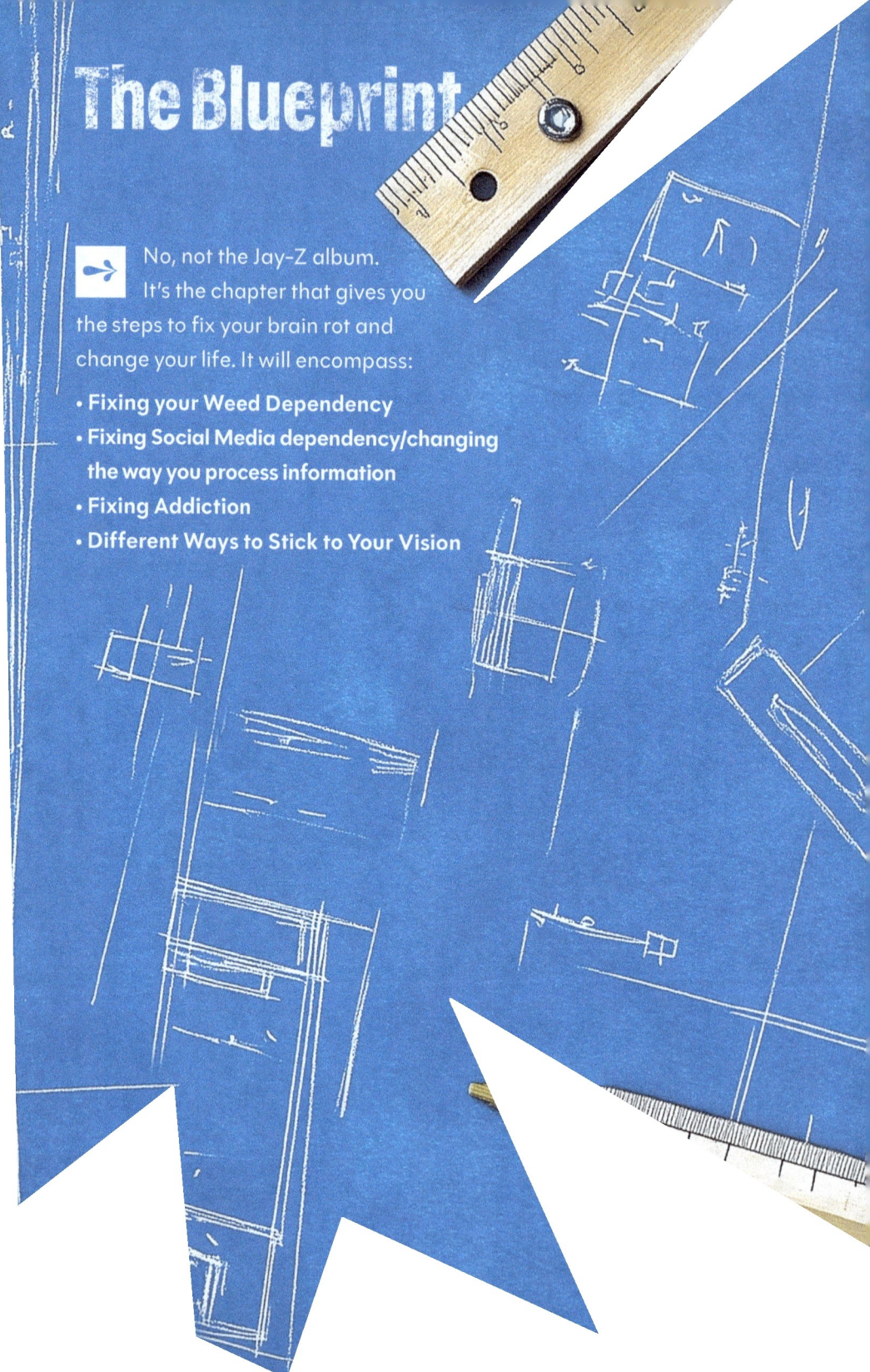

No, not the Jay-Z album. It's the chapter that gives you the steps to fix your brain rot and change your life. It will encompass:

- Fixing your Weed Dependency
- Fixing Social Media dependency/changing the way you process information
- Fixing Addiction
- Different Ways to Stick to Your Vision

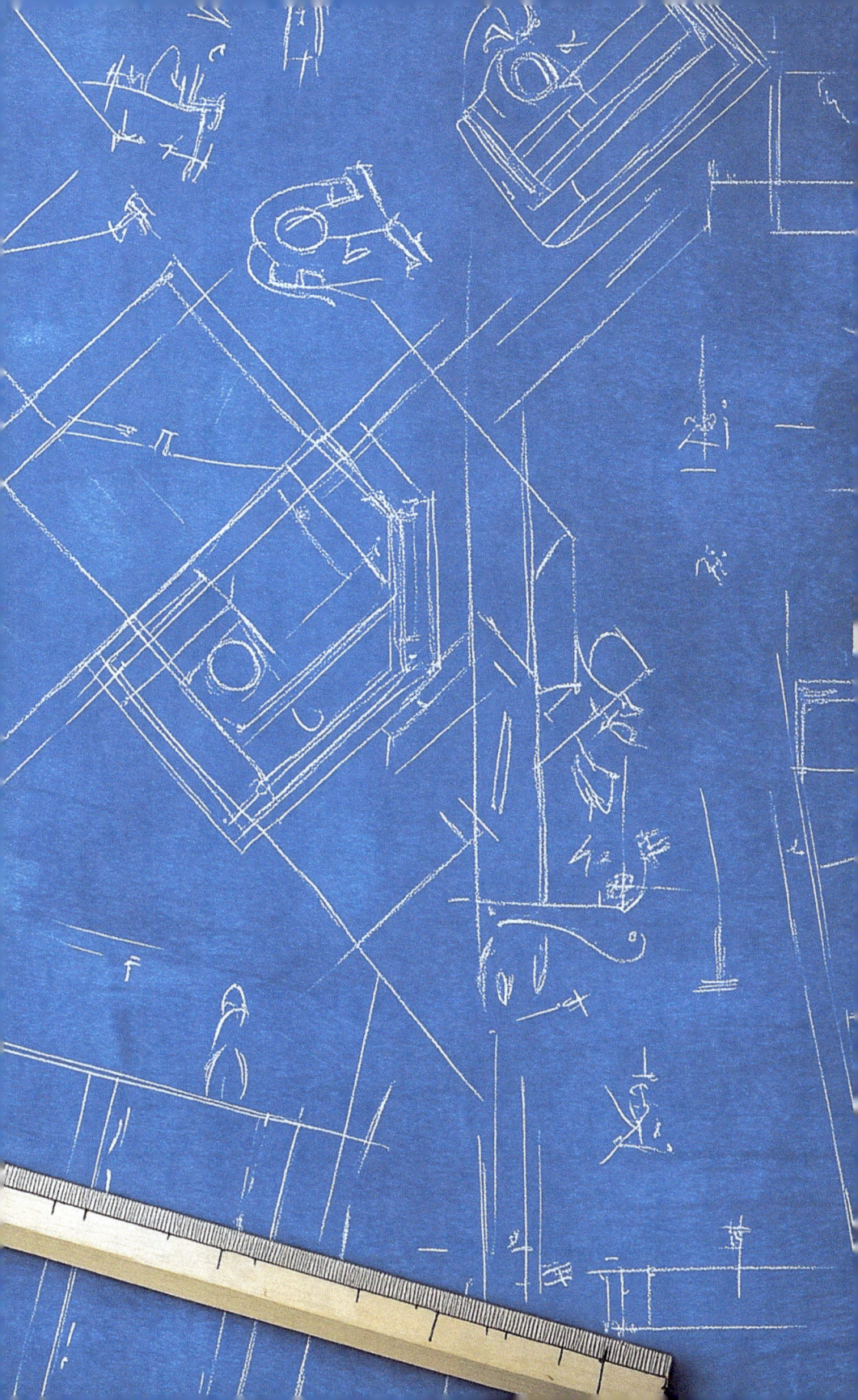

Sticking to the Plan

By now, you've developed your purpose, your identity, and your why. You have a vision of the future, a plan for the present, and now you just need to break it down.

Remember you are still you. Even as you reflect on your life's future, even in your newfound motivation and excitement, you are still a master procrastinator, someone who can't kick your addictions cold turkey. If you attempt to attack your vision without a plan, it will remain just a vision. If you follow a clear, intentional path, your vision will become a reality. And that's what I'm here for: to give you the path you can follow in a simple and effective format.

There are hundreds of methods, ideas, and practices to kick your weed, social media addiction to the side. But if I share each and every one of them, smoke would start coming out of your ears.

The difference between those methods and the ones I will share with you is that they're simple. They're tailored toward our generation.

Know that the tried-and-true methods do come in tiers. A method that works in the beginning may not be as effective toward the end of your vision, and vice versa. For example, maintaining a calendar to schedule your different priorities and activities is incredibly useful. At the beginning of enacting your vision, this is not easy to create. Yes, organizing your day down to a T with a calendar is an amazing way to structure your life. But if TikTok is the first thing you open when you wake up, and you're the type of person to submit your assignments at 11:58 p.m., do you really trust yourself to stick to a Google calendar? Hell naw.

Some solutions are timeless, but some solutions must change with the times. Due to the content we consume, our age groups have to innovate and find ways to accommodate our attention spans. It doesn't take long to focus on another train of thought and put down the book. That's exactly why I structured these steps in a way that, even if you are at rock bottom and feel your worst, it'll get you up and make you feel somewhat accomplished. I have created not just methods, but a framework, a habit builder, and a perspective shift that will fix that brain rot of yours to become a productive machine. Each step is tailored to your vision so you use them to accomplish what you never thought possible. If you feel motivated to combine steps, feel free to do so and be even more productive.

Phase 1:

I discovered this phase while trying to fix my own brain rot. I coined the method "7 Minutes, 7 Days."

Half the battle to accomplish anything is getting started. It's easy to exaggerate how demanding an activity will be. We imagine how long it will take us, and how difficult it will be, and we decide not to proceed. For example, you've dedicated yourself to going to the gym, but it's 6 a.m., and it's leg day. You stayed up till midnight watching TikTok, and now you're considering a rest day instead. The hardest part is deciding to go and start the first couple of exercises. Afterward, the sets that follow aren't as difficult as you expected.

Once you begin a task, you feel just a little more motivated to see it all the way through. But getting to the point of starting feels like hell. It's daunting, and mentally straining sometimes. Believe me, I know.

We hear the typical advice when people say, "You gotta do it, even if you don't feel like it. It's hard, but you'll be glad you did." Yes. Duh. We know that. But how do you get to the point of starting? What's your specific strategy or plan? That's where 7 Minutes, 7 Days comes in.

Every day, you will have a sliver of free time. I don't care if you're Joe Biden or Jeff Bezos. Everybody has a window of time. Within these windows, you can either slave your life away to Tik Tok or work on your vision.

You can't let your mind and emotions decide when to act; they will always choose comfort. Instead, you need to override your brain and act without even thinking about how difficult a task might be.

7 Minutes, 7 Days takes advantage of this. Here's how it works:

When you're scrolling on TikTok or Instagram, you'll probably have a thought along the way like, ▶

"I should really work on myself," or, "I should really lock-in."

It's at that moment that you have to act. The first step of the 7 Minutes, 7 Days strategy is the 5-4-3-2-1 countdown. First, go to the clock app on your phone and select a 7-minute countdown—but don't start it yet!

Once the timer is there, at that moment you will count down and say out loud, "Three, two, one, *go!*" It is crucial that in that moment you *don't* skip the countdown and that when you say "Go," you start the timer and *stand up*. Mel Robbins calls this the 5-Second Rule. The countdown stimulates the prefrontal cortex, which is responsible for decision-making.[25] This will automatically help you move from thinking to doing. That jolt will suddenly kickstart your mind to action. The countdown engages your prefrontal cortex and preps your brain for action.

For the next seven minutes, do anything that's related to your goal. And I mean quite literally *anything*. Make your bed. Drink your water. If it's the gym, put on workout clothes and fill your water bottle. If it's a clothing brand you want to start, then research Alibaba for suppliers. If it's getting better grades, open up that folder or binder and study your notes. Whatever it is, make sure those seven minutes are laser-focused.

As you do this, you will hit a point where the alarm rings. You've already committed to your seven minutes. You did what you had to do at that time. If you want to chill, chill. If you want to scroll, scroll.

But that's the beauty of those seven minutes. When you make progress on yourself, you don't want to stop. That alarm is going to ring, but you'll want to keep going. Maybe research a couple more suppliers. Maybe the seven-minute alarm rang as soon as you were done putting on your gym clothes. Because you want to better yourself, you tell yourself, "I've already started, might as well see it through."

Let me walk you through a scenario to show you how this would look.

1 You're in bed watching Zeddywill TikToks and Fanum GTA Roleplays, and you've noticed you've been there a while…watching Nara Smith make her 16th Ciabatta roll from scratch and JerseyJoe dislocate his hips.

2 You reflect on your vision, and what you want to accomplish, and you think, "Man, I need to act. This trade school application won't finish itself."

3 At that moment, you go to your clock app, and set the timer for seven minutes, but don't press it just yet. You stare at it, dreading what comes next.

4 But you decide you're going to act. You say out loud, "5-4-3-2-1, Go!" You jolt up, confused because your brain felt lazy just moments before, but your body feels like it moved on its own.

5 For seven minutes, you promise yourself to be laser-focused. You research schools for your trade of choice (maybe just one, given the short timeframe) and you look through their mission statement. You decide you might want to tour.

6 Then, the alarm rings. The seven minutes are over. You're free to stop. But you've already started the work. You even got to the point where you're considering adding 3-4 more schools.

7 You decide you want to keep working. You research two more schools. Maybe three. You get a list of recruiters you want to email. Those seven minutes turn into forty-five. At that point, you decide to call it a day. Now you feel proud of yourself for having accomplished something noteworthy.

That is the beauty of 7 Minutes, 7 Days. We all have seven minutes a day to choose to do something. After you've spent those seven minutes being productive, you somehow feel like you owe it to yourself to see it through. The countdown is what kicks it off, but the desire to continue is ultimately your own.

You must commit to this for seven days in a row. **Every seven days is a streak of one.** It's important to understand that when trying to accomplish the best version of yourself, it's a marathon, not a sprint, which is why you must chip away at your goals little by little every day. ▶

When Saturday rolls around, and you still decide to press that timer even though it's the weekend, imagine how much better you'd feel about yourself. If you prove that you can work on creating the life you want to live seven days a week with no breaks, you'll feel accomplished. Successful. Motivated to do more.

Phase 2: Animedoro (Pomodoro)

This study method has been popularized by the YouTuber Josh Chen. He made a powerful video titled, "How I Studied 600 Hours and Watched 300 Hours of Anime in 4 Months (The ULTIMATE Study Technique)."[26] Before watching, I was skeptical. How could you watch that much TV and still be focused? After I watched the video and saw how he broke it down, I was surprised his method didn't shoot up even more in popularity! (Of course, he is a medical student.)

His method is actually a twist on the traditional Pomodoro study technique. If you don't know what Pomodoro is, it's a time management method that involves 25-minute stretches of focused work followed by five-minute breaks. After four cycles of work intervals, longer breaks (15 to 30 minutes) are taken.

The Pomodoro method is a good way to be productive, but I understand how this may not be ideal for some. A five-minute break after a 25-minute grind period may feel too short for some. When I used the Pomodoro technique, my five-minute breaks turned to an hour every time without fail. You may need something more satisfying and rewarding.

Josh Chen incorporates the Pomodoro method while creating an altered version of it. He uses the fact that most anime/sitcom episodes are 20 minutes (when you take away the intro and the outro). So he suggests you combine this with Pomodoro by **working for a 45-minute interval and taking a break for that 20 minutes to watch your favorite anime/sitcom. That means for every 2 ¼ hours of work you do, you watch one hour of a show, and for every 22 and ½ hours of work, you watch 10 hours of a show.**

Though the method is called Animedoro, you don't have to watch Naruto save Sasuke from the Akatsuki or Itadori piece up Mahito in Shibuya. Sitcoms like *New Girl* and *Brooklyn Nine-Nine* are 20 minutes in length too, so you can watch that instead.

But what if you want to watch an hour-long show?

After all, *Power Book II* and *The Boys* are each an hour long. You want to see if Monet can protect Cane or maybe find out if Homelander ever took out Butcher and his team.

I created these simple time splits to ensure that you do the *minimum* amount of work to enjoy a longer break.

- **40 Minute Grind:**
  20 Minute Break
- **80 Minute Grind:**
  40 Minute Break
- **2-Hour Grind:**
  1-Hour Break
- **4-Hour Grind:**
  2-Hour Break

It's important that when you take your breaks, you don't go above the allowed time slot. If 20 minutes is your break, 20 minutes is your break. You will only cheat yourself by going above what you've earned.

So, as you're creating your trade school applications or trying to break into Wall Street through your interview preps, remember this framework when you feel the procrastination itch coming. Combine this with the 7 Minutes, 7 Days method to get the most out of your productivity.

Phase 3: Time Blocking

My goal is to simplify productivity for you. Time blocking is the last and final phase. Why? Because you have to work your way up to be successful at it.

After you've spent a decent amount of time on 7 Minutes, 7 Days, and incorporated Aminedoro into your routine, you may notice you've reached some milestones toward your vision. By now, you've probably noticed you need to be more organized. This is where time blocking comes in.

Time blocking is carving out times on your calendar when you commit to a certain task. In my experience, this is the pinnacle of productivity. The more tasks you can include in a day, the better. However, it may be too much and too fast to fully adopt it into your life, so we'll apply it in stages.

I created another realistic framework for you to build up to a full schedule of time blocking by starting with the basics. We'll progressively add tasks in each stage.

Phase 3.1:

Simple Time Blocking: (social media time, grind time, and hobby time)

When you're time blocking for the first time, just these three are enough: Social Media Time, Grind Time, and Hobby Time.

When starting out, time block just three days a week. Every Sunday, you will sit by your computer, open Google Calendar, or a physical calendar, and time block for social media time, grind time, and hobby time for three specific days.

Make sure to time block social media for either one time block for an hour-and-a-half or three time blocks for 30 minutes each. Keep it light. No more than that.

For grind time, if you feel like the 7 Minutes, 7 Days method is working for you, keep at it. But at some point, you will need more structure in your life. You'll have more of an idea of what times you're free after practicing the 7 Minutes, 7 Days method. As you gear up and take your life more seriously, your time blocks for grind time must be three hours at a minimum during any part of the day. (This includes breaks if you're doing the Animedoro method.)

For hobbies, find an hour in the day to do the things you love. Whether it's the gym, learning guitar, Duolingo, etc., this will help you stay focused on your goals while getting a much-needed refreshment from the work you've put in.

Phase 3.2

Strategic Time Blocking. (fluff and serious)

My goal is to make productivity simple for you, and I believe a balanced amount of social media time, grind time, and hobby time are perfect time blocks for anybody to live a productive life. The Phase 3.1 model I gave you is a very simplified and beginner-friendly version of time blocking. Once you've grasped Phase 3.1, move into Phase 3.2, "Fluff and Serious."

It's at this point we move on from time blocking just 3 days a week to now time blocking Mon–Fri.

Now is the time to incorporate time for fluff. *What is fluff, exactly?* Put simply, it's the annoying tasks you have to get out of the way before you get your day started.

The fluff buffer is a 30–45 minute buffer at the start of your day where you: breathe in, breathe out, meditate, drink coffee, check emails, read the news, edit your calendar, fill up your water bottle, and do just about anything else you feel will make your day easier.

After the fluff buffer, it's time to move on to the serious buffers. Serious buffers are the time blocks I mentioned before where you devote to working a minimum of three hours (including breaks). In Phase 3.1 you committed to doing it once a day (during grind time), but in Phase 3.2, you are now going to do it 2x a day.

The work you do will be dependent on your current focus and goals. If you're a student, grind time may look like completing all your homework and studying for an upcoming exam. If you're an entrepreneur, grind time may look like researching the process of creating an LLC and a business plan. Outside of work blocks, you can follow the 3.1 framework and schedule gym times, social media times, and hobby times as well.

Six hours of grinding may sound like a lot, but all that time will push you far ahead of what you've accomplished so far. Your vision is possible if you invest that amount of time every day. On Sunday, plan out Monday through Friday until you know exactly what your schedule during the week will look like. The time you'll spend grinding, pursuing a hobby, and scrolling on your phone will all be calculated, as it should be.

Once you've developed your ability to time block, you can advance to other efficient versions of the method. Consider these strategies if they match your workflow better.

Day Theming

Day theming involves you dedicating each day to a different type of work, to knock out every task related to the theme. For example, you can use Sunday for planning, Monday for studying, Tuesday for assignments, Wednesday for researching, Thursday for test prep, Friday for socializing, and Saturday for big projects you'd like to complete. Maybe throw hobbies in there as well. Feel free to repeat anything on any day (ex. making Monday and Tuesday test prep). Day theming allows you to take a deep dive and focus, finishing an entire project you set out to do. There might be some overlap, but to really hone this time-blocking method, you'll want to establish one major focus.

Bi-Modal Time Blocking

Next, you have bi-modal time blocking. Sounds complicated but is actually quite simple. Bi-modal time blocking refers to alternating between blocks of "deep work" and "shallow work." Deep work involves tasks that take up all your energy and require intense focus (deep reading, interview prep, or trade school applications), while shallow work is for more routine tasks (responding to emails, grocery runs, or journaling). This method gives you the ability to mix high-concentration tasks (like writing or coding) with low-effort activities (like responding to emails or doing paperwork). The beauty of this method is that your brain has a chance to recover from deep work by temporarily stopping high-bandwidth activities. Your brain can then rest from potentially overloading itself.

Day Theming

Time Batching

Another method is time batching. It refers to grouping similar tasks that you would complete in one sitting, rather than alternating between many different assignments. The plus side of this method is that you don't have to switch to other types of work repeatedly. In turn, this helps your brain function at a higher capacity—it's not bogged down by too many processes. If you've ever worked at a job with too many roles and responsibilities, you know brain rot will kick in without mercy! Rapidly and repetitively switching from task to task is just not good for the brain long term. Remember, your brain doesn't have a clear all tabs button. Every distraction is taking away from your focus.

Time batching helps alleviate the hustle and bustle of too much activity. For example, if you're starting a clothing brand, you can time-batch all your design tasks. Dedicate a block of time to focus only on creating mockups, refining your logo, and finalizing your brand's colors, instead of interrupting your flow state by switching between designing one minute and managing other tasks like social media the next. You can batch administrative tasks, for example, responding to emails, making phone calls, and/or filling out information for your future business.

Time Boxing

And lastly, we have a method known as time boxing. I mention time boxing at the end because it applies most to perfectionists. For some, it may be tempting to use the limits of time blocking that I mentioned as just a suggestion. You may find yourself two hours past what you set out for grind time. You've been working on it all day, and you have no designated end in sight. *It has to be done right! It has to be done perfectly!* But now, your grind time is getting in the way of other activities that help your brain recover. *That's all right! I'm being productive, though, so it's a good thing!*

I hate to break it to you, but you're wrong. Although it may seem like the more work you put in the better, the dangers of becoming a workaholic have similar effects to those of weed, social media, and content. It may not lead to permanent brain rot, but the more you overload your brain, the less sleep you get, and the lack of relaxing activities you participate in, the more you fry your brain.

Here is an example of a time-boxed schedule:

7:00 AM – 8:00 AM:

Morning Routine & Breakfast

Start the day by waking up early. Use this hour for personal time—showering, getting dressed, and having a healthy breakfast to get energized for the day.

8:00 AM – 9:00 AM:

Design/Creative Work for Clothing Brand and/or Applications

Before lectures start, spend an hour sketching hoodie designs, refining logos, or creating mockups on design software like Adobe Illustrator or Canva. If you're in school and are gunning for a job, this time can look like interview prepping for internships.

9:00 AM – 12:00 PM:

Morning Lectures/Classes

Focus entirely on your classes. Engage with the material, take notes, and participate in discussions or group work as needed.

12:00 PM – 12:30 PM:

Lunch Break

Use this break for lunch and to relax. Step away from academics and clothing brand work for a bit to recharge.

12:30 PM – 3:00 PM:

Afternoon Lectures/Classes

Attend your remaining classes for the day. Stay focused and take in as much as you can from these sessions.

3:00 PM – 4:00 PM:

Supplier Research and/or Cold Emailing

After class, use this hour to research potential suppliers on platforms like Alibaba, or start creating your brand's packaging and tags. Look into supplier reviews, minimum order quantities, and pricing for your hoodies. If you're job hunting, this time could look more like cold emailing to get introductions at the company of your choice.

4:00 PM – 5:00 PM:

Social Media Planning for Clothing Brand and/or Linkedin Searching.

Work on creating a social media presence. Plan out Instagram, TikTok, or Pinterest posts that reflect your brand's aesthetic. Draft captions, schedule posts, and engage with relevant communities. For the job hunters, this time could look like job hunting on Linkedin, and maximizing your connections.

5:00 PM – 6:00 PM:
Break & Dinner

Take a well-deserved break to eat dinner and relax. No girl-dinners. This is also a good time to connect with friends, unwind with a show, or scroll through social media.

6:00 PM – 7:30 PM:
Product & Market Research and/or Job Research

Focus on researching trends in streetwear, hoodie designs, and the market competition. Study other clothing brands and note what's working for them in terms of designs, marketing, and customer engagement. Again, for the job-hunting folks, use this time to search for different company cultures and research company initiatives that align with your long-term goals.

7:30 PM – 9:00 PM:
Study Session (Catch Up on Schoolwork)

Dedicate this time to any school assignments, readings, or exam prep. Keep this window free from distractions to focus on your academic priorities.

9:00 PM – 9:30 PM:
Short Break

Step away from your work to relax. Grab a snack, chat with friends, or take a walk. Make a TikTok (if they haven't banned it already)

9:30 PM – 10:30PM:
Branding Strategy & Email Outreach and/or More Interview Prep

Use this time for business tasks related to your clothing brand. Send emails to potential suppliers, contact manufacturers for quotes, or brainstorm ideas for branding and marketing strategies. If you're job hunting, prepare for your last interview of the day.

10:30 PM – 11:00 PM:
Night Routine & Wind Down

Wind down for the night with your personal routine. Reflect on the day's progress, mentally recharge, and prepare for the next day.

No matter how near you are to "perfecting" it, you quit as soon as the time expires. You either proceed to the next assignment or take a break to refuel. This kind of precise time management helps you maintain a balanced schedule, keeps you productive, and helps you avoid burnout. The goal is to maintain quality without wearing out your mind, not how much time you spend on it.

You need a well-balanced schedule, which is exactly why I created the time blocks the way I did. You need time to rest. You need time to breathe. Watch a Twitch stream. This is why time blocking helps you to be productive, but it also prevents you from overworking. You need breaks from high-concentration tasks. Setting time limits for each task and stopping once you've reached that limit is the key to creating an equilibrium, homeostasis, and a healthy brain. It will prevent perfectionism and frustration from getting the best of you. Rest up. After six hours of grind time, you deserve it.

Now that we've discussed the steps of productivity in order (from 7 Minutes, 7 Days to time blocking), it's your turn to apply these methods. Your dopamine hit used to come from weed, social media, and content, but now, productivity is your high. After a few months of time blocking, you won't even recognize yourself! The difference will be night and day.

Setting time limits for each task
& stopping once you've reached
that limit is the key to creating
an equilibrium & healthy brain

What About My Addiction(s)?

→ You've spent your time discovering your identity, purpose, and your "why." You now understand what drives your addictive behaviors and have directed your energy toward your vision instead. You are a productive machine.

But what if those addictions still get in the way? What if I'm still smoking, what if I'm still scrolling, what if I'm still consuming content? What if they affect my grind?

Cue me again. Not to worry. I have a blueprint for tackling your vision and tapering off those behaviors. Let's take a closer look.

Weed

To preface this section, let me start off by saying that I get that people's relationship to weed is different across the board. Some of you feel like you just can't cut it out completely. You might believe weed is harmless, despite the evidence proving its negative long-term consequences.

I recognize the importance of freedom, that you will ultimately decide how you want to live your life. I can sit here and tell you your habits might have detrimental effects on you, but if you disagree, there's nothing I can do to change your mind. For your sake, I'll teach you how to incorporate weed in your life in a healthier way or phase it out slowly.

First, which of the following statements best describes you:

1 I don't want to stop completely, but I want to reduce the amount I smoke.

2 I want to fully quit.

No matter where you fall, this advice is for people at all stages of their addictions.

High CBD/Low THC Products

The weed chapter earlier explains the effects of marijuana on the brain. But if you need a refresher, two of the most well-known compounds in weed are THC (tetrahydrocannabinol) and CBD (cannabidiol).

THC is the primary psychoactive compound in cannabis. This is what makes you feel "high." It binds to cannabinoid receptors in the brain, particularly the CB1 receptors, leading to the classic "high" associated with marijuana use.

Unlike THC, CBD does not produce a high. It interacts with the body's endocannabinoid system differently, primarily affecting CB2 receptors, which are more abundant in the immune system.[27] This leads to various therapeutic benefits without the high that THC brings. That's why if you go to a store, like a Walmart, you'll see CBD in certain shampoos, lotions, or even teas.

CBD has a calming effect on the brain. It can help with anxiety and stress. It also influences serotonin receptors, contributing to its anti-anxiety and mood-stabilizing properties.

If you want to fully quit weed, quitting cold turkey is the worst way to do it. If you've gotten to the point where you want to quit, chances are you have some type of dependency upon it.

Relapse occurs because the brain and body have become used to the presence of THC. When THC is suddenly removed, the endocannabinoid system, which regulates mood, sleep, appetite, and pain, is thrown out of balance. Quitting cold turkey will cause severe withdrawal symptoms, which is why it's paramount to come off it slowly.

Using high CBD/low THC products allows for a gradual reduction in THC consumption, minimizing withdrawal symptoms and reducing the likelihood of relapse.

Start with a Balanced Ratio: Begin by using products that have a balanced ratio of THC to CBD in your routine. For instance, if you are currently using high THC products, switch to a 1:1 THC to CBD ratio product. This helps to start reducing the psychoactive effects while still providing some of the familiar sensations.

Gradually Increase CBD

Over time, gradually increase the CBD content while decreasing the THC content in the products you use. Move from a 1:1 ratio to a 1:2 (THC to CBD) ratio after a month, then to 1:3 the month after, and so on. This slow transition helps your body adapt to lower levels of THC without experiencing severe withdrawal symptoms.

Monitor and Adjust:

Pay close attention to how your body and mind respond to the changes.

If you experience significant discomfort or cravings, slow down the transition process. The goal is to reduce THC intake at a pace that feels manageable and sustainable.

For those who want to keep smoking, this advice is practical for you, too. You may enjoy the high but hate the brain fog, laziness, and lack of productivity that comes with the THC. It's possible to find a balance where you can still enjoy the benefits of cannabis without sacrificing your productivity and cognitive function.

6 Week T-Breaks

If you've smoked before, you've probably heard of T-Breaks. If not, it quite literally means tolerance breaks—periods of time when you abstain from smoking. These breaks allow your body and brain to reset, reducing your tolerance to THC and making the effects of cannabis more potent when you resume use.

T-Breaks can be beneficial for maintaining a healthy relationship with cannabis because you give your endocannabinoid system a chance to rebalance. The length of your T-Breaks matters, though.

Word on the street is that T-Breaks should ideally last at least 21 days because it takes about that long for THC to leave your body completely. THC is lipophilic, meaning it binds to fat cells and is stored in the body's fat tissues.[28] As a result, it takes longer to be metabolized and eliminated from the system compared to other substances (if you've ever failed a drug test, now you know why). During those 21 days, your body has the opportunity to flush out the THC deposits, which helps to significantly lower your tolerance.

Your tolerance will decrease, and you'll better understand your relationship with it. What I propose is a six-week T-Break (42 days) rather than a three-week T-Break (21 days).

I say this because, after the three-week period, your body is now in a state of reset. Most of the THC has left your body. So, spend three weeks waiting for that THC to filtrate out of your body. Then spend another three weeks in a THC-free state to adjust your life without it and see if you decide to smoke afterward.

Now, there's not a perfect science to the amount of time to refrain from weed after your initial three weeks of sobriety. Three weeks is arbitrary. I only picked it because it's double the time of the recommended T-break. However, six weeks could be eight. It could be ten. It could be twenty. The important part is spending time in that THC-free state to avoid your tolerance increasing to unprecedented levels.

If you smoke as an escape, I highly encourage you to remain in that THC-free state. It is even more important that you refrain from weed because doing so gives you an opportunity to tackle your problems with a clearer mind.

Focus on Your Vision

Whenever you feel like it's just not worth it, feel tempted to give up on sobriety, consider throwing in the towel and going back to a life of brain rot, remember your vision. There's a reason those exercises were so extensive. The exercises provided you with a north star, an exciting reminder of a better future.

Take any necessary steps to minimize the temptation to smoke. Create the conditions around you that support positive behavior. If hanging out with certain friends requires smoking weed, maybe they weren't really friends to begin with. If spending copious amounts of time alone gives you the urge to smoke, surround yourself with people who support you by giving up or reducing weed use. If boredom strikes and the ganja gremlins are screaming your name, find ways to be more productive and time-efficient.

Keep your vision as a constant reminder, so when you do get the urge to smoke, you're reminded of all the work that needs to be done and the success you've already achieved. You should be ready to fall asleep at the end of each day because you accomplished so much.

The substances are going to phase out of your life the more progress you make. Your goals will no longer align with the desire to smoke weed, and saying "no" will become easier.

Sleep Tips

Routine Comes Last!

You've incorrectly thought that having a bedtime routine is the only missing piece in fixing your sleep schedule. It's not your fault. This piece of misinformation has been so normalized that people have accepted it as fact. A bedtime routine is incredibly useful ONLY if you've addressed the other root problems. What are they?

Improve your Waking Hours

How do you spend your waking hours? Well, Dr. Alok Kanojia, also known as Dr. K or HealthyGamerGG on YouTube says fixing your sleep schedules starts with addressing how we spend our waking hours rather than focusing solely on bedtime routines.[29]

In our day to day, our brains need adequate waking activity to accumulate fatigue signals like melatonin and adenosine. Adenosine is a neurotransmitter in the brain that helps you regulate your sleep and accumulates during your waking hours. There's a natural sleep window that we have where if we miss it, it becomes increasingly harder to fall asleep. Dr. K states that most people miss their optimal sleep window, typically between 9 PM and 10 PM, due to impulse control issues like technology, television, checking our phones, over-watching YouTube documentaries, and any action that takes away from our sleep. This leads to sleep procrastination. The brain's frontal lobes, responsible for impulse control, become tired, making it harder to resist distractions and go to sleep.

So, how can we guarantee our waking hours are adequate enough to promote good sleep?

1 Take out the Trash & Learn New Things & Be Bored:

How often does your mind race? When I had sleep troubles, it was every day and every night. Dr. K states that when we go to sleep in an anxious state, it makes it harder for us to achieve restfulness. Practice being bored throughout the day. Yes, boredom. I know it sounds impossible given the current technological landscape but you need to give your brain adequate amounts of time in the day to sort out its thoughts. Another thing that helps with sleep is learning. Thinking requires a lot of energy and your brain expends a lot of it through its mind racing. Sleep is the time when your short-term memory becomes encoded into your long-term memory. The more you learn in a day, whether it be a skill or a language, the more your brain needs to encode in its slumber. A day of learning will send signals throughout your body that'll induce sleep so your brain has time to sufficiently sort through short-term and long-term memory. Simply sitting down and allowing your mind to race throughout the day, learning new things, and being bored can do wonders for your sleep. Journaling can also help organize the brain vomit that's racing around as well.

❷ Exercise:

I'm sure you've heard this one before. Exercise increases the production of melatonin, regulates your body temperature, and changes the levels of stress hormones in your brain. Weightlifting in particular creates small muscle tears that send signals to your muscles, bones, and your brain to induce sleepiness. Muscles are repaired in sleep, so your body will induce sleep to aid in that repair.

What themes are we seeing? What you do in your waking hours contributes to your quality of sleep. The more you use your brain and body, the easier it will be to fall asleep. Routine comes last. If you address the bedtime routine aspect before your daily routine, that breeds a recipe for disaster.

Medication:

Many people claim they use weed to sleep, but studies have shown that marijuana is not a shortcut to deep, restful sleep. The underlying causes of your lack of peaceful sleep are likely due to your self-sabotage, trauma, and escapism. Even melatonin should be a last resort to sleep. Not only can you become dependent on it, but it is also a hormone and metabolism disruptor when taken too frequently. Too much melatonin can negatively affect your insulin, which helps control your blood sugar. Additionally, it can affect the balance of cortisol (stress hormone), estrogen, and testosterone in your body.[29] Once you've addressed your waking hours and need a supplement to aid with sleep, try magnesium glycinate, 350 to 500 mg an hour or two before sleep (first consult with a doctor).[30] Unless trips to the bathroom are your thing, I would avoid or at least consult with a doctor if you want to buy magnesium citrate instead. Those are typically taken before a colonoscopy to make sure your region is clear. ▶

Magnesium plays a role in the activation of gamma-aminobutyric acid (GABA), a neurotransmitter that promotes relaxation and sleep. GABA inhibits neural activity, helping to calm the nervous system and induce sleep.[30] Magnesium is also responsible for the production of serotonin, a precursor to melatonin, the hormone that regulates sleep-wake cycles. By precursor, I mean serotonin gets converted into melatonin, the sleep hormone. This conversion happens in the pineal gland, signaling your body that it's time to sleep. Adequate levels of serotonin contribute to better sleep by promoting feelings of well-being and relaxation.[30]

Shifting Your Mindstate:

Again. Routine Comes Last! Address your waking hours first before you address your bedtime routine.

When you walk into your room, your hand moves toward the light switch without a thought. You probably take off your shoes, change into your inside clothes, and get settled. You've been doing it for so long that these actions are driven by your subconscious. Your mindstate even shifts as you transition from the outside world to the comfort of your room.

The same logic can apply to creating a bedtime routine. In college, I've heard people say many times, "I can't study in my dorm, or else I'd find my way to my bed and sleep." We associate our bed with sleeping because every night, putting our head on a pillow signals to our brain that we want to relax or go to sleep.

But what do we do instead? Doomscroll instead of sleeping while the phone's light messes up our circadian rhythm. Binge until the sun comes up, messing up our sleep schedule. Half the battle is developing a routine. The other half is doing it every day until it sticks. Substances like Magnesium only go so far if you're not treating your routine with respect.

Here are some tips on developing a routine and sticking with it

Develop a Bedtime Routine:

Every night, find a list of actions to take to prepare for sleep, in addition to the usual brushing your teeth and CeraVe night cleanse. One way to do this is to optimize your sleep environment around the time you're ready to go to sleep.

Optimize Your Sleep Environment:

• CHARGE YOUR PHONE:

The first thing you must put down is your phone. Light itself strongly affects your circadian rhythms. When you wake up, the sun sets up a chain of cycles in your body that signals it's daytime.[31] Blue light, which is a wavelength component of daylight, has the strongest effect, which is why you must put your phone or any screens away 30 minutes before bed.

• TEA:

Tea can be an incredible sleep aid. There are a lot of caffeine-free sleepytime teas that hit just as hard as melatonin. My personal favorite is Chamomile. Not only is it tasty with a teaspoon of honey, it has Apigenin, which is a compound with sleepy-time effects that binds to the same GABA receptors magnesium does in the brain.[32]

• DARKNESS:

Blackout curtains or eye masks can help block out extra light and prime your environment for sleep. After you're done brushing your teeth, putting away your phone, and brewing your tea, move your curtains together as a next step.

• TEMPERATURE:

Keep your room at a temperature that induces sleep. Around 65°F/18°C is ideal for most people.

• GET INTO BED:

Even if you're not the most tired, the act of getting into bed will send a signal to your brain that you're ready to sleep. Fight against the urge to check your phone. Count sheep for all I care. Do this every day until the action becomes as automatic as turning on a light switch.

P.S: Another source of sleep problems can be a bad mattress. Mattress toppers are a great alternative to good mattresses, which can be quite expensive. Sometimes, the difference between good sleep and great sleep is really good memory foam.

Social Media

Disclaimer: I'm not going to suggest deleting social media entirely. Why? Because it's so deeply embedded in our lives that we rely on it for updates, news, and entertainment. Social media has its value, just as much as it has its downsides. Like most things, it's about moderation—too much of anything isn't good, and social media is no exception. The issue with saying, "I'm quitting social media for good," is that it isolates you from the world. It cuts you off from valuable education and resources. Most importantly, it sends the message that the only way you can control this urge is by eliminating it completely, rather than learning to integrate it into your life in a balanced, healthy way. You've probably tried social media blockers and ignored the limits every time. It's not sustainable. The method I'll share won't just help you manage your social media use—it'll make you smarter and more intentional with your time.

In this section, we will learn ways to manage our social media use, a topic heavily promoted by the YouTube video "How I'm Learning to Think Clearly" by Joseph Tsar.[33] That video changed the way I viewed social media and became a major motivation in my writing this book. I realized brain rot goes deeper than the number of little TikTok or YouTube Shorts sound bites you repeat in a day, or the brain fog you feel after scrolling through social media until the sun comes up. It not only affects you in the present, but it literally changes the way your brain processes information.

TikTok, YouTube Shorts, Twitter, Instagram Reels, and other content have conditioned us to consume media in very short, digestible pieces. This rapid dissemination of information has trained our brains to focus for only short amounts of time, continually resetting to receive new content. We develop a low tolerance for longer viewings, videos, and readings. To put it in colloquial terms, our attention spans are cooked.

We consume posts, videos, or articles without critically considering others' conclusions and the way they got there. We go from one thinkpiece to the next, not understanding the thought processes and motivations behind each post. We develop a surface-level grasp of the ideas presented without being exposed to the steps and reasoning behind them. Have you ever scrolled on Twitter and seen a tweet get a ridiculous amount of likes, but the tweet itself is either untrue or misunderstood? That's the outcome of consuming without thinking.

Take some of your recent conversations with friends, for example. What conversations have you had lately?

Really focus on the way you engaged versus the way the other person engaged. How long did you stay on a certain topic?

- **Dyran:** Man, I saw this TikTok the other day talking about how Bronny James is only in the league because of his dad.
- **Ayosike:** Yeah, that's ridiculous.
- **Dyran:** Yeah, that's crazy right? He could've just bummed it out with his dad's money, but he's actively trying to make it for himself.
- **Ayosike:** Mmmhm, he's grinding.
- **Dyran:** Yeah, that's crazy.
- **Ayosike:** Yup, for sure.
  (40-second pause)
- **Dyran:** Aight, I'm gonna head out.
- **Ayosike:** Okay. See you, bro.

Here is an example of a delusional person without an original thought:

- **Natalie:**
  If my partner doesn't make $650,000 a year minimum, he can't be my man.
- **Ray:** Why $650,000 a year minimum? Why that specific number?
- **Natalie:**
  I don't know. I heard it on a TikTok, and it just made sense.
- **Ray:** ....

Now, let's say you're networking and meeting people for the first time.

- **Philemon:** Hey, nice to meet you. My name is Philemon.
- **Roger:** My name is Roger. Nice to meet you. How's it been?
- **Philemon:** Not too bad. So, what do you do?
- **Roger:** I'm in computer engineering. I work at a FAANG.

- **Philemon:** Wow, interesting. Do you like what you do?
- **Roger:** Yeah, I can't complain. It pays the bills. I get to enjoy my hobbies.
- **Philemon:** Yeah, that's real.
  [pause]
- **Philemon:** So, what do you do for fun?
- **Roger:** I play 2K on the weekends. Maybe hit a jazz club. How about you?

- **Philemon:** I'm more of a football guy. The parlays hit more.
- **Roger:** I don't really watch football much, but I've been trying to get into it.
- **Philemon:** You should! It's fun to watch.
- **Roger:** Yeah, I bet it is.
  [pause]
- **Philemon:** So, how's the wife?
- **Roger:** I'm divorced.

I am not exaggerating these conversations for the sake of proving a point. I hear conversations that go exactly like this in my everyday life! There's never a real train of thought that is seen all the way through to the end. Why? All the short-term content we consume trains us to no longer engage in long forms of thought. Our brains are becoming the media we consume.

Think about your brain like a TikTok or an Instagram Reel. When you're done with the content, you swipe to the next; & in the same way, when it comes to conversations, you move on quickly from topic to topic with little to say about each. The time you spend on each topic is short because you've only consumed limited information on it. You're training your brain to focus for only 30-40 seconds at a time. We went from books to reels real quick.

So the phrases, "Damn, that's crazy," and "Wow, that's so cool," that you insert in the conversation are actually a buffer of time, a go-to tool you use to think about the next thing you're going to say. Your mind is likely playing catch up, trying to draw from everything you can think of to continue the conversation. When your brain can't formulate a coherent thought or contribute to the conversation in time, you feel the pressure of silence and awkwardness start to set in. Just like a TikTok, your mind swipes to the next conversation topic. You've conditioned yourself to only stay on a topic for a maximum of 40 seconds at a time.

This is why your conversations lack substance. You're so used to the dopamine rush of instant satisfaction that the slow gratification of good conversations no longer has the same effect. You'd rather be on TikTok than talking to someone. That's when you know that brain rot has set in. You're in need of a detox, a dramatic change to get your life back on track. To once again have a clear mind and experience real life.

If you suffer from brain rot, you likely regurgitate the internet more than any other source. It has become the ultimate authority of logic and reason in your mind. You quickly adopt opinions from celebrities or influencers without even evaluating or understanding them fully! With so many opinions on the internet, people who depend on social media for their information have only a surface-level understanding of many topics. They know a little about a lot of subjects but have no deep understanding of what matters most to them.

We were never meant to consume this amount of media, to see these many ideas in a given day. It's only a matter of time before it overloads your brain. When a new topic is introduced in a conversation, you find that you can't even think clearly. You're too busy trying to digest the hundreds or thousands of ideas you saw on TikTok to be able to say the right thing.

For instance, if someone mentions trauma bonding and you watch a 40-second TikTok video about it, you may mention it.

"Hey, I watched a TikTok about trauma. She said because the internet is so widespread, people have a platform to share their problems. Whether it's relationship problems, home problems, or anything that's troubling them. When we watch these people share their experiences, we sometimes internalize their trauma, looking for issues that don't exist in our lives, but subconsciously creating them because we're paranoid."

This is an excellent thinkpiece on social media that requires a lot more nuance than a two-minute video. But outside of that quick video that explained that concept, you can't expand on it after you brought it up—your brain hasn't had time to think critically about what was said. You decided to watch another TikTok after the video on trauma bonding, so your perspective on the topic went *poof*. You continued from video to video until your brain fogged up with information; your ideas and thoughts were not streamlined. Now that excellent thinkpiece is tangled up in your brain like headphones after you leave 'em in your pocket for too long.

What I'm about to say will go against the grain, but it will shed light on the issue of social media and who is to blame.

Social media itself is not the problem. The way you engage with it is the problem. ▶

I've actually used TikTok for some personal growth, knowledge, and education. I've learned a rich amount of helpful information from highly intelligent creators. The inspiration for this actually came from many of the videos I've watched on the platform. In some instances, I learned more from TikTok than my college-level courses.

The same goes for Twitter. Outside of the 'rent-is-due' hypotheticals I see on that app daily (should your partner pay your entire rent?), I've bookmarked and saved thinkpieces on social issues that have changed my way of thinking. Social media is like a cafeteria. You may be in a different grade, but once it's lunchtime, everybody comes together. The bookworms and the delinquents.

You may be surprised to hear me describe the positive side of social media (if used appropriately). We just spent the whole time learning about the detrimental effects of doom scrolling. *Now you're trying to tell me I'm in the clear?*

It comes down to one word: balance. It's the balance of when and how to use social media that gets the best of us. We must decide whether to use it sparingly or extensively and how we interact with it.

I'd be lying if I said social media was not a vice for me as well. The ways in which I engaged with it were not healthy. I found myself trying to process a thousand videos I swiped through in a seven-hour binge period. At that point, I felt my brain rotting away.

I just shared both examples of my social media use to demonstrate that you can reap the benefits of social media while also preventing binging and brain rot. It's now time to provide a framework to establish a healthy relationship with social media instead of quitting it cold turkey.

Create a note on your notes app or buy a notebook and write down any topic you found interesting in a TikTok video you watched. Next, engage with that topic for at least a week. Engage intentionally.

For example, I saw an interesting thinkpiece on Twitter a while back.

When movies depict Italian crime, people refer to it as the Golden Era of Organized Crime. When black people are depicted in criminal acts, it's often referred to as a cultural issue and a race problem.

I used to see interesting thinkpieces like this and scroll away immediately. This time, I wrote it in my notes app and took a week to engage with it. I rewatched *Scarface* and *The Godfather*, and took notes in my notes app about depictions of crime. I rewatched *Boyz n Tha Hood* and looked up movie critics and the differences in which the movies were interpreted. I went to TikTok, watched videos on reinforced stereotypes, and educated myself on biases. On YouTube, I found videos on author and journalist Ta-Nehisi Coates and listened to his takes on prejudice.

I didn't stop there. I found content from people I disagreed with. It was important for me to understand their perspectives to put my new knowledge into context. I started doing this every week for every new thinkpiece or interesting thought I came across. Over time, my mind started to organize itself. It felt like my brain was creating file cabinets to organize my thoughts. I heard the Claratin jingle in my mind—*I can see clearly now the rot is gone.*

Once you start engaging with media this way, you'll sharpen your critical thinking, activate your mental faculties, reverse the effects of brain rot, and provide clarity. If you practice this every week, you'll be on your way to becoming the individual of the hour, the life of the party with something to talk about all the time. By engaging in mentally stimulating conversations, provoking deep thought, and building a genuine connection with the people around you, you'll have successful friendships and relationships.

Focusing and researching a topic introduced to you by social media for a week can single handedly cure your social media brain rot. It will organize the fog in your brain. I know. It sounds so basic...but it works! I owe it to Joseph Tsar for introducing this method.

If you've (unfortunately) been on the podcast side of TikTok or the thinkpiece side of Twitter, then you've seen some opinions that ranged from, "Wow, this is genius," to, "This man/woman should never pick up a mic again." The problem is that we go through this content so rapidly that we adopt these opinions as our own without thinking it through for ourselves.

You may be scrolling on Twitter and/or TikTok, watching people share their bad experiences, whether it be in the corporate world, relationships, etc., and hold negative sentiments toward a particular gender. Maybe you watched the entire "Who TF Did I Marry?" TikTok series and decided you'll never trust another man again. On the surface, it seems playful, but this has long-term consequences because what you're doing is internalizing other people's trauma as your own. When you speak about the corporate scene or the dating world, you start drawing from other people's experiences instead of your own.

Let's visualize this advice through a brain map to help you better contextualize the words.

1

The brain rot implications are far and wide. I want to use the concept of a brain map to show you how it's damaging you and how to fix it.

This is your brain.

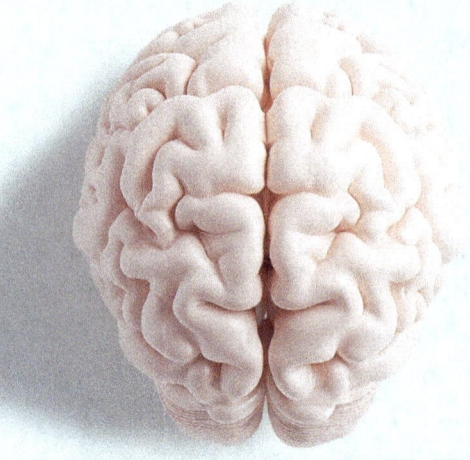

There is a ton of information that your brain stores. And everyday, it stores even more through your life experiences, the things you engage with, etc.

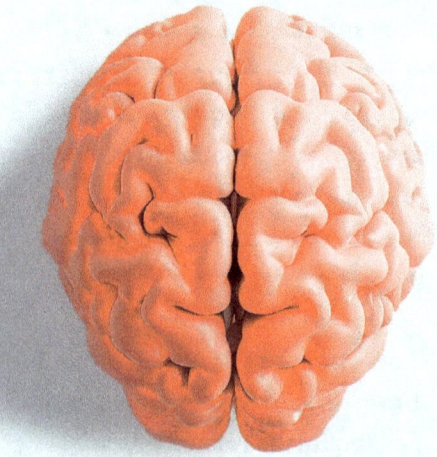

2

Everytime you open Tik Tok or engage with an idea, it gets processed and stored in your brain.

WHAT DO YOU BRING TO THE TABLE

PODCASTS

FOOD RECIPES

TOXIC EXES

RELATIONSHIPS

IT'S 7PM FRIDAY. IT'S 95 DEGREES

However, the information you engage with in a day is a lot.

So when you're done with your 7 hour TikTok binge, you swiped through about 1,000 videos. Your brain is trying to process bits and pieces of what you managed to remember from these TikToks. But, the information is so much that it goes into overdrive.

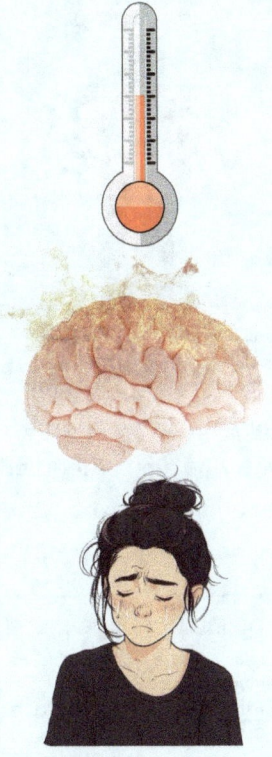

This contributes to the fog or fried feeling you feel after you're done with a binge, which makes you feel horrible. And when you try to engage in conversation, your brain is trying to pull from so many different areas that haven't been thought out fully. It'll look something like this.

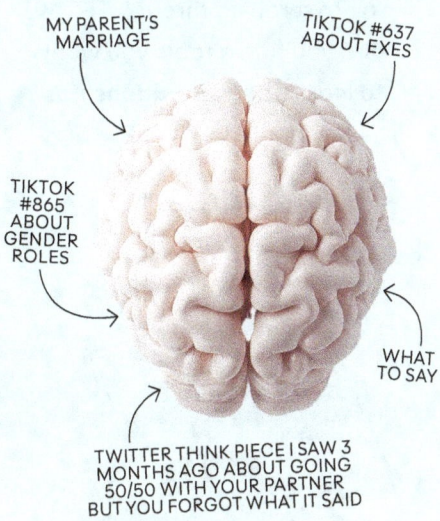

MY PARENT'S MARRIAGE

TIKTOK #637 ABOUT EXES

TIKTOK #865 ABOUT GENDER ROLES

WHAT TO SAY

TWITTER THINK PIECE I SAW 3 MONTHS AGO ABOUT GOING 50/50 WITH YOUR PARTNER BUT YOU FORGOT WHAT IT SAID

Because your brain hasn't had the time to flesh out these TikToks and ideas you've engaged with, you can't speak in confidence to a lot fo the topics that's brought up because it's surface level. Like a TikTok, your mind is swiping through these 30 second videos of incomplete thought, which leads you to speak about incomplete thoughts.

And the more this continues, the worse it gets. Your brain rot will only continue to worsen.

So how do you fix it?

You have to engage with the things you find interesting for more than that 40 second interval. Intentional engagement. I will show you how to incorporate this into your life step by step. ▶

You're scrolling through TikTok and you find a topic you want to learn about. **Relationships should be 50/50.**

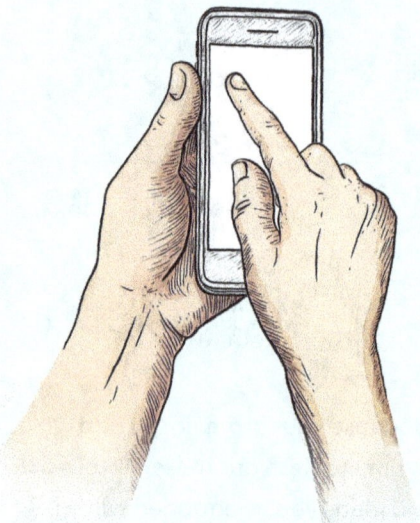

You either put it in your Notes app or you write it down in your notebook. Write down everything you feel about this topic/statement to avoid blindly believing it.

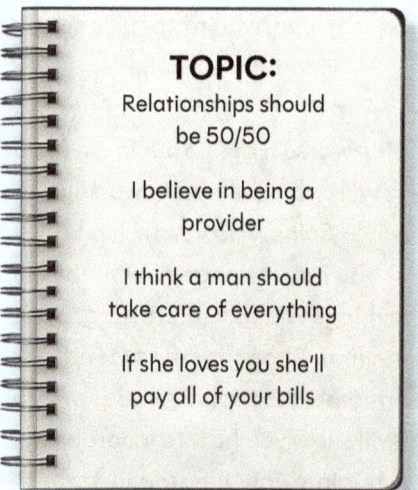

TOPIC:
Relationships should be 50/50

I believe in being a provider

I think a man should take care of everything

If she loves you she'll pay all of your bills

Throughout the week, at least once a day for a minimum of 5 days, find a youtube video, podcast, article, etc related to the topic. Read about it and engage with it to learn more about it. Actually take in the information.

Everyday, go back to your notes and update it with what you've learned or change up what you no longer believe.

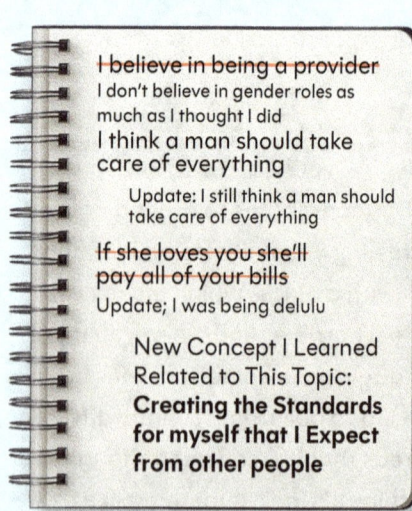

~~I believe in being a provider~~
I don't believe in gender roles as much as I thought I did
I think a man should take care of everything
  Update: I still think a man should take care of everything
~~If she loves you she'll pay all of your bills~~
Update; I was being delulu

New Concept I Learned Related to This Topic:
Creating the Standards for myself that I Expect from other people

Once you're done with the week, go back to your notes and see how much knowledge you added to what you found interesting.

Throughout the week, you should be adding topics to your notebook from the TikToks you found interesting. Once you finish one, move on to the next one the next week.

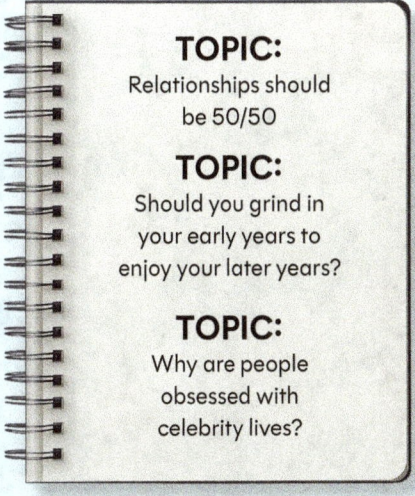

TOPIC:
Relationships should be 50/50

TOPIC:
Should you grind in your early years to enjoy your later years?

TOPIC:
Why are people obsessed with celebrity lives?

Once you do this for a while, instead of your thought process and conversations looking like this.

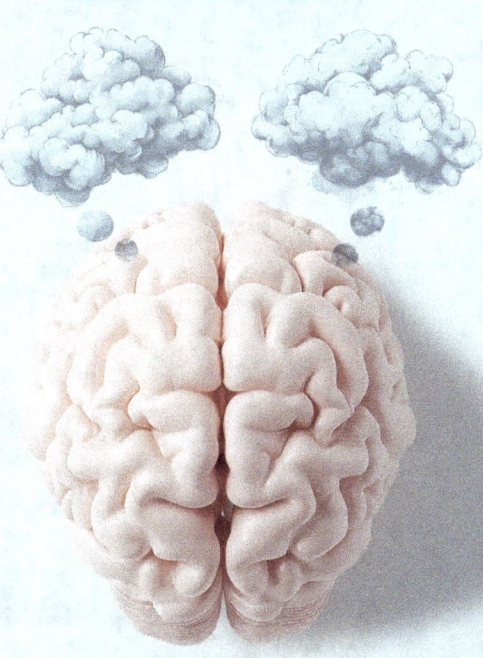

They instead look like this. And you can offer more perspectives on the situation.

TOPIC: RELATIONSHIPS

SAYING RELATIONSHIPS SHOULD BE 50/50 IS CLOSE MINDED BECAUSE THERE ARE TIMES WHERE YOU'RE AT 30 & YOU NEED YOUR PARTNER TO BE AT 70, & VICE VERSA

IS IT THAT YOU STRUGGLE WITH ROMANCE OR DO YOU NOT LOVE YOUR PARTNER AS MUCH AS YOU THINK YOU DO

IT'S IMPORTANT TO NOT PLACE EXPECTATIONS THAT WE CAN'T MEET OURSELVES

ARE YOU LOOKING FOR LOVE BECAUSE YOU SEEK COMPANISONSHIP OR ARE YOU LOOKING FOR LOVE TO FILL A VOID

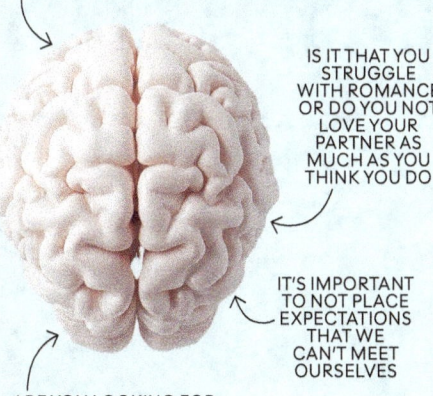

It's easy to just say that social media isn't worth your time. It's easy to download an app to block Instagram and TikTok. You could've just told yourself to limit your screen time. Stay away from social media. Focus on your vision. You've heard that all before, though, right? You've tried it, and what happened? It didn't work.

You decided to delete Instagram because you wanted to go on a "dopamine detox." But after day three, you feel the social media itch, and the only way to scratch it is by watching reels. You think to yourself, *I'm HIM. I'll stick it through*. Three days turn to seven. Seven days turns into three weeks. You're proud of how long you've gone without social media. You think, *let me download the app again. I think I'm good.*

But then what happens? You fall right back into the same cycle. *Damn. Not this again.*

Don't get me wrong. I am a big advocate for social media breaks, but many who undergo a "detox" can't get back to a healthy social media checking habit afterward.

Social media detoxes aren't the sole solution to healthy social media engagement. Intentional engagement with key topics is the best way to tackle brain rot and social media addiction. We can now have a relationship with these platforms without villainizing the apps. You first have to untrain your mind from the short-form content of social media by proactively engaging with it. This will better establish you as a critical thinker, giving you clarity and a wealth of knowledge to create meaningful conversations.

The more you engage, think, and reflect, the less brain rot will consume your mind. You'll have the mental energy and resources to really get after the vision you've been meaning to chase.

Pitfalls & Recommendations

Congratulations. You made it to the last part.

This section is a word of advice explaining the common pitfalls you'll experience, and the traps to avoid when you're on your path to change your life.

The Peaks and Valleys

Understand that all change is difficult. You're not going to experience a 180 in your life right away. There are stages to change, and you must be aware of them before embarking on your transformative journey.

I would hate for you to be so invested in your vision, and then suddenly stop at a point that's necessary for change. I don't want the weight of success to overwhelm you because you're lost in the process. Let's go through the phases one by one so you know what to expect and how to overcome them.

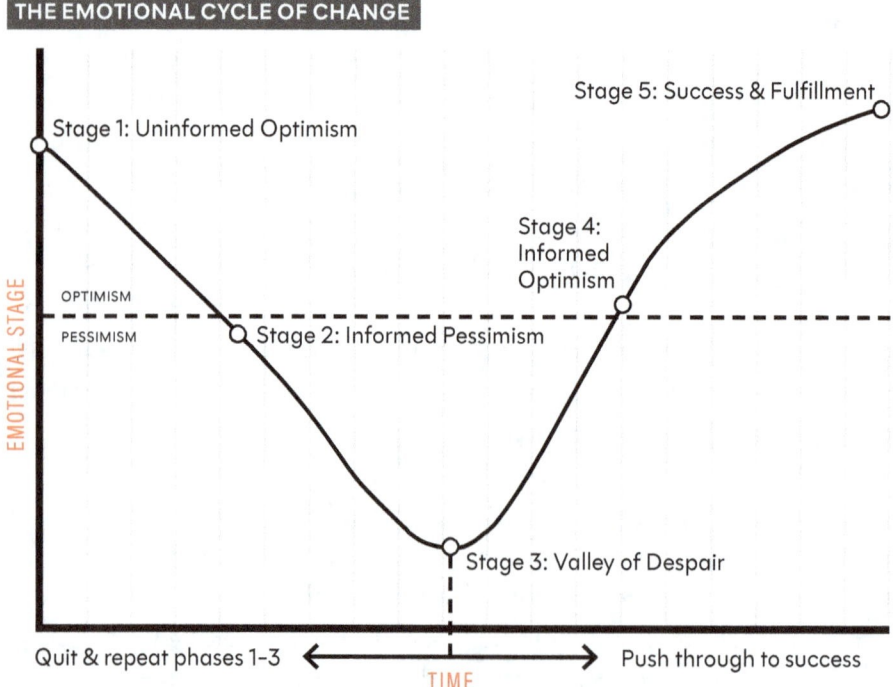

THE EMOTIONAL CYCLE OF CHANGE

Stage 1: Uninformed Optimism

Stage 5: Success & Fulfillment

Stage 4: Informed Optimism

OPTIMISM

PESSIMISM Stage 2: Informed Pessimism

EMOTIONAL STAGE

Stage 3: Valley of Despair

Quit & repeat phases 1–3 ← → Push through to success

TIME

1 Uninformed Optimism

This is when you first get that idea. Clothing brand. YouTube. Becoming the next Kai Cenat. Opening up a car shop.

You're excited, giddy, envisioning what the future can be. At this stage, you have no idea the amount of work it'll take to get there or how you're going to get started. You don't care! It's going to happen! You buy that equipment, you set up that ring light, and you start recording. Time to upload the first video! You're just happy to start.

2 Informed Pessimism

You start learning the reality of what it takes to make it, and discouragement starts to set in. Not enough to make you quit, but enough to make you question yourself. You uploaded a couple of videos. You get 100 views on your first upload. Damn.

You're still excited, though, so you keep uploading, but your next ten uploads get just ten views...combined! You start learning about the YouTube algorithms, tags, etc. You're beginning to realize there's a lot you don't know. It weighs on you heavily, but you carry on.

3 Valley of Despair

You've been at it for a while. A heavily concerted effort. But nothing seems to be taking off. You fall into deep pits of sadness, and you think you're just not cut out for success. Your videos aren't gaining traction. You've tried all types of thumbnails, and clickbait titles, but nothing you try is working. You even stop uploading for a while because it's got you down. The one time you actually try to do something for yourself and give it your all, nothing. No vision in sight. No major goals were achieved. You become extremely depressed and fall back to your old ways.

The valley of despair has taken many souls. Robbed people of their dreams before they saw their success. They could be on the verge of a breakthrough, but they never get there because they gave up. Those who end up here usually don't make it to the next stage. They see everything as falling apart or bound to fail.

I don't want the valley of despair to take you, too. This is a crucial part of change. If you feel extremely down about your perceived lack of success, just know the valley comes first, and success awaits on the other side for those who persevere. ▶

④ Informed Optimism

The depression slowly becomes replaced with the realization that wallowing in sadness won't get you closer to your ideal life.

You see the ring light on your table, and you're reminded of the days you used to grind, believing you would get thousands of views on every video. You decide to pick up that camera again and get back to work. This time, though, you're using a more calculated approach. First, you do more research into the topics you don't know. Then, you check your videos again to see where you went wrong. "Oh, I shouldn't have titled it this way," or, "The thumbnail doesn't fit my target audience." You start making slight tweaks and adjustments because you understand that if you take care of the small stuff, the big things inevitably take care of themselves.

Now that you've researched your market, area of expertise, and put it into practice, you stick to your vision, knowing success is on the verge. It took longer than first expected, but you're okay with that because you have the end in mind.

⑤ Success and Fulfillment

The small changes you make day by day are seeing bigger wins. You look back now, knowing your expectations are all over the place. You wanted to be Kai Cenat, Fanum, and them right out of the gate. You didn't realize it's going to take some time to get there. You've learned to enjoy the small wins. You enjoy seeing those 1,000 views increase to 5,000.

Your subscribers and supporters are slowly but surely growing. Your success is not sporadic anymore, but rather strategically contained. You fall in love with the journey knowing that you are currently living out your past prayers.

Success and fulfillment will help you to stomach the storms that still come along the way. You're hitting milestones and marks that you never thought you'd reach.

The Validation Trap

If you've ever heard somebody tell you to keep your goals to yourself, there could be multiple reasons why.

Some people are afraid that if you share your goals with other people, it'll jinx you or invite the evil eye. It'll stop your goals from being achieved. And even worse, somebody could run with your idea and sell your product before your business has a chance to take off.

Although those are valid reasons not to share your vision, I believe you should not speak a word of your goals, or keep your circle tight for a different reason. If you mention your goals before you accomplish them, you might fall into what's called a validation trap.

Validation is a double-edged sword. We want to be recognized for what we do, but often, we seek this praise in every aspect of our lives. When you were younger, you sought validation from your friends and teachers. When you're older, you seek validation from your bosses.

Why? It could come from the void formed because your parents never told you they were proud of you, and you try to fill that with praise from others. It could be from a lack of good friends who support you and lift you up. Whatever it is, the need for validation is real.

When you tell people about your goals and aspirations, it feels good. I'd say, a little too good. The dopamine spike you get after being praised for your goals is intoxicating.

That's exactly the problem we're trying to avoid. If you are receiving the reward of dopamine from others' compliments on your goals or vision, you're more focused on the praise than actually accomplishing them in the first place. Dopamine is a reward for doing something you're supposed to do. If you are receiving the reward before you accomplish the goal, your brain is tricked into feeling a sense of completion. This premature sense of achievement can sap your motivation and diminish your drive to put in the actual work required to achieve your goals. Your achievements can be delayed or ignored because you want to hear praise for your goals rather than accomplishing them and getting the reward of dopamine from your own efforts.

Over time, this can lead to a dangerous cycle: the satisfaction of sharing one's goals replaces the satisfaction of achieving them.

On top of that, you prioritize external expectations over internal expectations. ▶

When you start to share your goals with others, you may feel pressure to meet their expectations instead of focusing on your own intrinsic motivation. Instead of being driven by your passion and determination, you become more concerned about how your progress is perceived in the minds of others. This shift in focus can then lead to procrastination; the fear of not meeting other people's expectations can be paralyzing. Your goal becomes less about personal growth and more about receiving a pat on the back and a high-five from others.

External validation can be fleeting and inconsistent. Over time, others may lose interest in your goals, leaving you without the support you initially received. This can demotivate you and make it harder to stay committed to your objectives.

Take this scenario, for instance:

1. You think about how you have to lock in and become successful not only for yourself but for your family.
2. You see your mom coming home from a long shift, tired and exhausted. You think about the life you want to give your family.
3. You then look at your mom and say, "Mom, one day I'm going to put you in a house." You see her smile and light up. Her satisfaction is your satisfaction. Your dopamine levels are high. You feel motivated about the future.
4. Over time, the dopamine starts to come down. You start working on your vision and realize how far out from your goal you actually are.
5. The initial excitement fades, replaced by the daily grind and the slow, often frustrating progress. The goal you set begins to feel more distant, and the weight of the commitment starts to press on your shoulders.
6. You find yourself less motivated. The high from that moment you promised your mom a home dissipates. Reality sets in.
7. You begin to question yourself and your abilities. The pressure of others' expectations makes the journey more daunting than you hoped. *I can't let my mom down!* That fear looms large.
8. Instead of drawing strength from your promise, you feel burdened by it. The path to achieving your goal becomes a source of stress rather than inspiration. The initial dopamine rush that made you feel unstoppable now feels nonexistent.

This scenario serves as a reminder that the reward should come from the small wins you're making every day toward your vision...the validation you receive from other people will not sustain you.

There are instances where sharing your goals is good, but only if what you seek isn't validation, but rather accountability, encouragement, advice, and connections. I have a group chat with five of the most innovative friends I've ever met. Every day, we bounce around ideas, our drafts for our newsletters, and business ideas that are insanely creative. Every day, we make sure to hold ourselves accountable, encourage each other when times get tough, give practical advice, and leverage our connections to help our ideas grow.

I'm a huge advocate for keeping your circle small and speaking about your ideas intentionally. Seeking validation will only keep you going back for it while accountability, encouragement, advice, and connections allow you to see your ideas from a level state of mind.

The "Action" Trap

People call it pseudo-productivity; I call it the action trap.

Whatever you want to call it, beware of it.

We are all guilty of this. Performing tasks that make us feel like we are doing something important or making progress, but we aren't making a dent. Checking your emails a little bit too long. Spending time on the PowerPoint formatting rather than the slide content.

Why do we focus on what's not important? Well, first, it's a form of procrastination. Living the life we want requires doing hard work. Sometimes we brush those tasks aside, and we do the easy things instead. It takes work to get dressed and drive to the gym. *Why don't I just do ten pushups and call it a day?* All of those emails you're reading are a lot easier on your mind than doing research on the business you've been telling yourself you want to start.

The effort it takes to achieve success can't be overstated. You have to put in the work. You can't nitpick the action items you want to do every day and be upset that you're not where you want to be.

Success is the ultimate promise we make to ourselves; we owe it to our dreams to give nothing less than 100%.

All or Nothing

You want to change, but urgency without a plan is burnout waiting to happen.

If changing your life could happen overnight, then there was no need for these exercises. There was no need to learn how to build yourself slowly to make sure your foundation was strong enough to weather the storm. You would've just done it. However, I'm sure you know through your trials and errors that trying to change everything all at once only puts you in a worse place than you were before.

Flooring the pedal is how you run out of gas.

Forcing the pace is how you fall behind.

Sprinting through life is how you miss the journey.

Changing your life can't be an all-or-nothing approach, because life itself isn't all or nothing. It's a long journey that's kind to those who understand that patience is a virtue.

Remember, don't look for the light at the end of the tunnel. Embrace the darkness and build your own light in your journey.

"One step at a time. One punch at a time. One round at a time." – Rocky Balboa

Self-Aware

This chapter is heavily inspired by a man who goes by the name of AG (Tiktok: @cookinglikeag).

You need to ask yourself a crucial question: Are you truly self-aware, or are you addicted to shame?

I'm sure you can easily list countless things you perceive as wrong with yourself: laziness, lack of motivation, lack of discipline—the list goes on. It is important to recognize where you fall short, but to dwell on them endlessly is to invite a storm of despair. True self-awareness is a delicate balance, an honest embrace of both your strengths and your weaknesses. When someone challenges your negative thought process and tries to uplift you, you incorrectly think you're self-aware. "Why lie to myself?" you say. "I know what I am. Why is it a crime to be honest about myself?"

But why is it a crime to love yourself too? **Self-awareness that only fixates on negative thoughts is self-destruction.** Focusing solely on your flaws will never lead you to success. You must recognize that you are worthy of success and love. Imperfections do not define the entirety of your being.

In your negative thoughts, you overlook the fact that you excel in many areas: compassion, creativity, drive, hunger, artistic vision, musical acumen, an eye for beauty, and the ability to love. You are unique, which means your success is unique too.

If thoughts about yourself are all negative, that implies shame, not self-awareness. When the best parts try to emerge, they are choked by this dome of despair. You shield yourself from criticism, believing that you need to be brutally honest to yourself before anyone else can voice your flaws, which you think is rooted in honesty. This self-imposed shield blinds you to your true potential and traps you in a cycle of self-doubt and insecurity. This creates a weak sense of self, making you easier to manipulate, sway, and less able to accept your beautiful qualities.

When you consume content from people who vocalize their shame publicly, it only amplifies your own. You internalize their shame, confessions, and experiences. You're listening to other people's problems, interpretations, and issues, and applying it to your life. You're shaping your frame of mind without even realizing it.

Security comes from trust, and the root of all trust is your belief in yourself. Show yourself why you are great and believe in your greatness. Pick up that canvas and believe you can surpass Basquiat. Pick up that rock and aim to soar higher than LeBron.

Most importantly, surround yourself with people who pour into you like a fountain, not a drain. People who see your vision and push you to believe in yourself because they recognize the greatness in you that you're blind to. They act as mirrors reflecting your best qualities back at you, helping you to see and internalize the best parts of yourself.

Now rise and let your light shine, and don't let anyone dim it because they think it's too bright.

The End

I Leave You with This.

There was a point in my life when I never thought I could write a book, let alone reach an audience. I had the thoughts: *Succeed. Make it.* However, the weight of people's expectations used to cripple me. I had no way to deal with it except to tough it out. Never talked to anyone about it. I dreamed of who I'd become when I was a child, but as I grew, that vision kept changing again and again, and I started to feel like the life I wanted was unattainable.

It was like nothing fell into place, no matter how hard I tried. I was rejected from life over and over. I was growing distant from my friends. My side hustles were falling apart, and I ended up in debt. Still, I had to put on a brave face and tough it out. Ball up top.

I went through it all. Everything that I mentioned to you. The social media addiction. The depression. The need for validation. The sudden realization that I can make my life bend to my will. The thought that life was in my hands and I was doing nothing about it. Letting the dice sit instead of rolling it. I was in a freeze state, unmotivated to act. I had a desire to change but the urge to do nothing at the same time. I felt a deep longing to change my circumstances, find success, and take control of a life that had no direction.

I fell into that cycle of brain rot, just like you. If it wasn't social media, it was running away from my responsibilities. I felt like there were experiences I never got to have growing up because of my fixation on school, so I sabotaged my responsibilities to experience them, not realizing I was hurting myself in the process. I thought I was making up for lost time, living the moments I felt I had missed out on. Each poor decision, each missing assignment, each party, and each kickback was a step further away from my goals and dreams. I was caught in a vicious cycle of wanting more out of life but choosing actions that only took me further from it. Self-sabotage became the way I coped, but it never provided any comfort.

I knew one thing, though. The life I wanted to live was going to be one I owned. I wanted to answer to myself and myself alone.

The day I established my vision was the day I changed. When I closed my eyes and imagined my ideal future,

I saw my mom in a house, siblings with their school paid for, homes being built in Senegal, and scholarship funds being established by me. I saw myself traveling internationally, giving motivational speeches, building businesses with my friends, and living out my dreams and hobbies. It lit a fire under me that has yet to go out.

Whenever I had an idea, I acted on it. Whenever I had a vision, I wrote it down. Through my failures, I understood how special I was. How unique my perspective is. How when I put pen to paper, my execution and style are one of one. To get to the point where I can say that about myself took years of self-doubt to overcome. I understood that your life will arrive where your mind frequently visits, and I chose to keep the doors of doubt locked, and the key thrown away. Doubt is a killer of dreams, and belief is a sower of seeds.

Believe in yourself. Speak about yourself as if you are one of a kind. Because you are. You offer the world what no one else does. A 100% unique individual from everyone else with an identity, purpose, and a "why" that only you can figure out. When you discover those three, you will overcome your fears. You will overcome your anxiety about the future. You will let go of your trauma and find escape in the things that get you closer to your dreams. You will let the world see you for who you are rather than who they want you to be. You will be successful. You *will* be successful.

There is a life you're put into, then there's a life you choose. Life is too short to choose a perspective where you're losing. Speak power into yourself as words have a way of manifesting. You have to think you are and say it proud before you see what you're truly capable of. You have to be before you become.

If I can take myself from the darkest pits of hell and write a book that will impact millions; if I can roll the dice and create the life I desire, why can't you? On the opposite side of your fear is everything you need. Go out there and go after it. You owe it to yourself.

Reach Out

I love thoughtful emails. If you need advice or someone to talk to, reach out either one of these two emails.
cureyourbusiness@gmail.com
papediopbusiness@gmail.com

Instagram: @pape_jr
Follow me to check out what I'm doing next, or to talk about anything your heart desires.

Youtube: @PapePKD
I'll be more active on YouTube I promise. That's where I post life advice, and vlogs about my life

Twitter: PapePKD
Get my follower count up please or else Elon will think it's a bot acccount

Reddit: r/CureYourBrainRot
This will be our community. A place to share how everyday, you chose the cure instead of the poison.

Substack: @igetpape
Follow me on substack to see my writing journey, thoughts, and messages along the way.
   I'll always be easy to reach and easy to talk to. Enigmas are losers.

Sources

1. "Abdaal. 2024. "You're Destroying Your Mind - How to Control Dopamine." YouTube. June 18, 2024. https://www.youtube.com/watch?v=tjjqyiHczc-c&t=632s&ab_channel=AliAbdaal.

2. Stanford Medicine. 2024. "Understanding the Teen Brain." Stanfordchildrens.org. 2024. https://www.stanfordchildrens.org/en/topic/default?id=understanding-the-teen-brain-1-3051.

3. Cherry, Kendra. "How Neuroplasticity Works." *Verywell Mind*, 2024, www.verywellmind.com/what-is-brain-plasticity-2794886. Accessed 14 Oct. 2024.

4. Ellerbeck, Stefan. 2022. "Nearly Half of US Teens Use the Social Media 'Almost Constantly.'" World Economic Forum. August 30, 2022. https://www.weforum.org/agenda/2022/08/social-media-internet-online-teenagers-screens-us/.

5. JOHNSON, CARLA K. 2024. "Daily Marijuana Use Outpaces Daily Drinking in the US, a New Study Says." AP News. May 22, 2024. https://apnews.com/article/marijuana-cannabis-alcohol-drinking-daily-use-b91c2c5957fdb2d48e6616c3baa14c13.

6. Hill, Kevin, and Michael Hsu. 2022. "Cognitive Effects in Midlife of Long-Term Cannabis Use - Harvard Health." Harvard Health. June 14, 2022. https://www.health.harvard.edu/blog/cognitive-effects-of-long-term-cannabis-use-in-midlife-202206142760.

7. Metricool. 2024. "TikTok Video Duration 2024 | Statista." Statista. 2024. https://www.statista.com/statistics/1485205/tiktok-video-duration/#:~:text=In%202024%2C%20TikTok%20accounts%20produced,TikTok%20was%2039%20seconds%20long..

8. Coy, Annamarie, and Nicko Estellado. 2024. "Internet Addiction Statistics: Prevalence and Impact - Addiction Group." Addiction Group. July 16, 2024. https://www.addictiongroup.org/resources/internet-addiction-statistics/.

9. Shanmugasundaram, Mathura, and Arunkumar Tamilarasu. 2023. "The Impact of Digital Technology, Social Media, and Artificial Intelligence on Cognitive Functions: A Review." *Frontiers in Cognition* 2 (November). https://doi.org/10.3389/fcogn.2023.1203077.

10. May, Kaitlyn E, and Anastasia D Elder. 2018. "Efficient, Helpful, or Distracting? A Literature Review of Media Multitasking in Relation to Academic Performance." *International Journal of Educational Technology in Higher Education* 15 (1). https://doi.org/10.1186/s41239-018-0096-z.

11. Shatz, Itmar. 2019. "Procrastination and Stress: How They're Connected and What to Do about Them – Solving Procrastination." Solvingprocrastination.com. 2019. https://solvingprocrastination.com/stress/.

12. Nodell, Bobbi . 2021. "75% of Sexual Assault Survivors Have PTSD One Month Later - UW Medicine | Newsroom." UW Medicine | Newsroom. July 20, 2021. https://newsroom.uw.edu/news-releases/75-sexual-assault-survivors-have-ptsd-one-month-later?

13. CrisisHouse. 2022. "What Is Trauma? - Crisis House." Crisis House. July 12, 2022. https://crisishouse.org/blog/what-is-trauma/?gad_=1&gclid=CjwKCAiA34S7BhAtEiwACZzv4Y0K65pg2LjeNlRW3CuqwwPxv51zegAcMc4AhtmpbnCijZgJ76lCbhoCOl4QAvD_BwE.

14. Downey, G., & Feldman, S. I. (1996). Rejection sensitivity as a mediator of the impact of childhood exposure to family violence on adult attachment behavior. *Development and Psychopathology, 8*(4), 789-813.

15. Shah, Nitin. 2024. "Understanding the Defense Mechanism of Identification with Aggressor." ICHARS. July 3, 2024. https://instituteofclinicalhypnosis.com/psychotherapy-coaching/psychodynamic-approach/understanding-the-defense-mechanism-of-identification-with-aggressor/.

16. "Id, Ego, & Superego | Freud & Examples." 2024. Simply Psychology. January 25, 2024. https://www.simplypsychology.org/psyche.html?

17. Gillette, Hope. 2019. "Signs You're Sabotaging Your Relationship and How to Stop." Psych Central. October 31, 2019. https://psychcentral.com/relationships/the-startling-reason-we-sabotage-love?

18. NeuroLaunch. 2024. "Self-Handicapping in Psychology: Exploring the Protective Behavior and Its Impact." NeuroLaunch.com. September 15, 2024. https://neurolaunch.com/self-handicapping-psychology/?

19. Smyth, Joshua M, Jillian A Johnson, Brandon J aAuer, Erik Lehman, Giampaolo Talamo, and Christopher N Sciamanna. 2018. "Online Positive Affect Journaling in the Improvement of Mental Distress and Well-Being in General Medical Patients with Elevated Anxiety Symptoms: A Preliminary Randomized Controlled Trial." *JMIR Mental Health* 5 (4): e11290–90. https://doi.org/10.2196/11290.

20. **Ware, B. (2012).** *The top five regrets of the dying: A life transformed by the dearly departing.* **Hay House.**

21. Sankar, Carol. 2017. "How the '5 Second Rule' Can Help You Fight the Urge to Proc rastinate." Inc.com. Inc. December 8, 2017. https://www.inc.com/carol-sankar/how-to-kick-habit-of-procrastination-in-5-seconds-according-to-a-bestselling-author-top-speaker.html.

22. Chen, J. (2021, January 11). *How I studied 600 hours and watched 300 hours of anime in 4 months (The ULTIMATE study technique)* [Video]. YouTube. https://www.youtube.com/watch?v=bUjGZJIgse0

23. The Editors of Readers Digest and Project CBD. 2022. "CBD & the Endocannabinoid System | Project CBD." Project CBD. September 5, 2022. https://projectcbd.org/science/cbd-the-endocannabinoid-system/?

24. University of Vermont. 2024. "T-Break: Take a Cannabis Tolerance Break | Center for Health and Wellbeing | the University of Vermont." Uvm.edu. 2024. https://www.uvm.edu/health/t-break-take-cannabis-tolerance-break?

25. Luchini, Justine . 2023. "Melatonin: Can Also Effect Your Hormones and Metabolism." Thirdzy. June 26, 2023. https://thirdzy.com/blogs/article/melatonin-hormones-and-metabolism? Kanojia. 2024. "Why Your Sleep Habits Aren't Healthy." YouTube. May 29, 2024. https://www.youtube.com/watch?v=cyKEfejsVps&ab_channel=HealthyGamerGG.

26. Blades, Nicole. 2024. "Does Magnesium Glycinate Really Help You Sleep Better?" WebMD. March 26, 2024. https://www.webmd.com/sleep-disorders/features/magnesium-glycinate-sleep?

27. Shultz, Cara. 2024. "Yes, Your Smartphone Is Keeping You from Sleeping — and Not Just Because You're Scrolling." People.com. 2024. https://people.com/

28. Yurcheshen, Michael, Martin Seehuus, and Wilfred Pigeon. 2015. "Updates on Nutraceutical Sleep Therapeutics and Investigational Research." *Evidence-Based Complementary and Alternative Medicine* 2015 (January): 1–9. https://doi.org/10.1155/2015/105256.

29. Tsar, J. (n.d.). *How I'm learning to think clearly* [Video]. YouTube. https://www.youtube.com/watch?v=WzsPAmeDykw&ab_channel=JosephTsar

30. Baragona, R., Battaglia, F., & Cucina, D. (2017). Empirical likelihood ratio in penalty form and the convex hull problem. *Statistical Methods and Applications, 26*(4), 507–529. https://doi.org/10.1007/s10260-017-0382-2

31. Clear, J. (2018). *Atomic habits: An easy & proven way to build good habits & break bad ones.* Avery.

32. Toronto.com. 2016. "Terry Crews Had Therapy for Porn Addiction." Toronto.com. February 25, 2016. https://www.toronto.com/things-to-do/terry-crews-had-therapy-for-porn-addiction/article_93c72d67-9f3a-56cc-8450-af2bfb4ac269.html.

www.ingramcontent.com/pod-product-compliance
Lightning Source LLC
Chambersburg PA
CBHW070909130626
46555CB00001B/70